A WOMAN YOUNG AND PASSIONATE

A COLLECTION OF ESSAYS,
EXCERPTS AND WRITINGS
ON EMILY BRONTË

By

MRS GASKELL,
VIRGINIA WOOLF,
JOHN COWPER POWYS,
ARTHUR SYMONS AND OTHERS

Copyright © 2019 Read & Co. Books

This edition is published by Read & Co. Books,
an imprint of Read Books Ltd.

This book is copyright and may not be reproduced or copied in any way without the express permission of the publisher in writing.

British Library Cataloguing-in-Publication Data
A catalogue record for this book is available
from the British Library.

www.readandcobooks.co.uk

CONTENTS

BIOGRAPHICAL NOTICE
OF ELLIS AND ACTON BELL
By Charlotte Brontë...................................5

CHARLOTTE AND EMILY BRONTË
By Millicent Fawcett 13

THE SISTERS BRONTË
By Mrs. Oliphant...................................24

HAWORTH
By Virginia Woolf..................................60

EMILY BRONTË
By Arthur Symons..................................65

EMILY BRONTË
By John Cowper Powys............................69

"JANE EYRE"
AND "WUTHERING HEIGHTS"
By Virginia Woolf..................................84

CHARLOTTE AND EMILY BRONTË
By Alice Meynell 91

THE CHALLENGE OF THE BRONTËS
By Edmund William Gosse 103

BIOGRAPHICAL NOTICE
OF ELLIS AND ACTON BELL

BY CHARLOTTE BRONTË

It has been thought that all the works published under the names of Currer, Ellis, and Acton Bell were, in reality, the production of one person. This mistake I endeavoured to rectify by a few words of disclaimer prefixed to the third edition of 'Jane Eyre.' These, too, it appears, failed to gain general credence, and now, on the occasion of a reprint of 'Wuthering Heights' and 'Agnes Grey,' I am advised distinctly to state how the case really stands.

Indeed, I feel myself that it is time the obscurity attending those two names - Ellis and Acton - was done away. The little mystery, which formerly yielded some harmless pleasure, has lost its interest; circumstances are changed. It becomes, then, my duty to explain briefly the origin and authorship of the books written by Currer, Ellis, and Acton Bell.

About five years ago, my two sisters and myself, after a somewhat prolonged period of separation, found ourselves reunited, and at home. Resident in a remote district, where education had made little progress, and where, consequently, there was no inducement to seek social intercourse beyond our own domestic circle, we were wholly dependent on ourselves and each other, on books and study, for the enjoyments and occupations of life. The highest stimulus, as well as the liveliest pleasure we had known from childhood upwards, lay in attempts at literary composition; formerly we used to show each other what we wrote, but of late years this habit of communication and consultation had been discontinued; hence it ensued, that we were mutually ignorant of the progress we might respectively have made.

One day, in the autumn of 1845, I accidentally lighted on a MS. volume of verse in my sister Emily's handwriting. Of course, I was not surprised, knowing that she could and did write verse: I looked it over, and something more than surprise seized me - a deep conviction that these were not common effusions, nor at all like the poetry women generally write. I thought them condensed and terse, vigorous and genuine. To my ear they had also a peculiar music - wild, melancholy, and elevating.

My sister Emily was not a person of demonstrative character, nor one on the recesses of whose mind and feelings even those nearest and dearest to her could, with impunity, intrude unlicensed; it took hours to reconcile her to the discovery I had made, and days to persuade her that such poems merited publication. I knew, however, that a mind like hers could not be without some latent spark of honourable ambition, and refused to be discouraged in my attempts to fan that spark to flame.

Meantime, my younger sister quietly produced some of her own compositions, intimating that, since Emily's had given me pleasure, I might like to look at hers. I could not but be a partial judge, yet I thought that these verses, too, had a sweet, sincere pathos of their own.

We had very early cherished the dream of one day becoming authors. This dream, never relinquished even when distance divided and absorbing tasks occupied us, now suddenly acquired strength and consistency: it took the character of a resolve. We agreed to arrange a small selection of our poems, and, if possible, to get them printed. Averse to personal publicity, we veiled our own names under those of Currer, Ellis, and Acton Bell; the ambiguous choice being dictated by a sort of conscientious scruple at assuming Christian names positively masculine, while we did not like to declare ourselves women, because - without at that time suspecting that our mode of writing and thinking was not what is called 'feminine' - we had a vague impression that authoresses are liable to be looked on with prejudice; we had noticed how critics sometimes use for their chastisement the weapon of personality, and for their reward, a flattery, which is not true praise.

The bringing out of our little book was hard work. As was to be expected, neither we nor our poems were at all wanted; but for this we had been prepared at the outset; though inexperienced ourselves, we had read the experience of others. The great puzzle lay in the difficulty of getting answers of any kind from the publishers to whom we applied. Being greatly harassed by this obstacle, I ventured to apply to the Messrs. Chambers, of Edinburgh, for a word of advice; *they* may have forgotten the circumstance, but *I* have not, for from them I received a brief and business-like, but civil and sensible reply, on which we acted, and at last made a way.

The book was printed: it is scarcely known, and all of it that merits to be known are the poems of Ellis Bell. The fixed conviction I held, and hold, of the worth of these poems has not indeed received the confirmation of much favourable criticism; but I must retain it notwithstanding.

Ill-success failed to crush us: the mere effort to succeed had given a wonderful zest to existence; it must be pursued. We each set to work on a prose tale: Ellis Bell produced 'Wuthering Heights,' Acton Bell 'Agnes Grey,' and Currer Bell also wrote a narrative in one volume. These MSS. were perseveringly obtruded upon various publishers for the space of a year and a half; usually, their fate was an ignominious and abrupt dismissal.

At last 'Wuthering Heights' and 'Agnes Grey' were accepted on terms somewhat impoverishing to the two authors; Currer Bell's book found acceptance nowhere, nor any acknowledgment of merit, so that something like the chill of despair began to invade her heart. As a forlorn hope, she tried one publishing house more - Messrs. Smith, Elder and Co. Ere long, in a much shorter space than that on which experience had taught her to calculate - there came a letter, which she opened in the dreary expectation of finding two hard, hopeless lines, intimating that Messr. Smith, Elder and Co. 'were not disposed to publish the MS.,' and, instead, she took out of the envelope a letter of two pages. She read it trembling. It declined, indeed, to publish that tale, for business reasons, but it discussed its merits and demerits so courteously, so considerately, in a spirit so rational, with a discrimination so enlightened, that this very refusal cheered the author better than a vulgarly expressed acceptance would have done. It was added, that a work in three volumes would meet with careful attention.

I was then just completing 'Jane Eyre,' at which I had been working while the one-volume tale was plodding its weary round in London: in three weeks I sent it off; friendly and skilful hands took it in. This was in the commencement of September, 1847; it came out before the close of October following, while 'Wuthering Heights' and 'Agnes Grey,' my sisters' works, which had already been in the press for months, still lingered under a different management.

They appeared at last. Critics failed to do them justice. The immature but very real powers revealed in 'Wuthering Heights' were scarcely recognised; its import and nature were misunderstood; the identity of its author was misrepresented; it was said that this was an earlier and ruder attempt of the same pen which had produced 'Jane Eyre.' Unjust and grievous error! We laughed at it at first, but I deeply lament it now. Hence, I fear, arose a prejudice against the book. That writer who could attempt to palm off an inferior and immature production under cover of one successful effort, must indeed be unduly eager after the secondary and sordid result of authorship, and pitiably indifferent to its true and honourable meed. If reviewers and the public truly believed this, no wonder that they looked darkly on the cheat.

Yet I must not be understood to make these things subject for reproach or complaint; I dare not do so; respect for my sister's memory forbids me. By her any such querulous manifestation would have been regarded as an unworthy and offensive weakness.

It is my duty, as well as my pleasure, to acknowledge one exception to the general rule of criticism. One writer, endowed with the keen vision and fine sympathies of genius, has discerned the real nature of 'Wuthering Heights,' and has, with equal accuracy, noted its beauties and touched on its faults. Too often do reviewers remind us of the mob of Astrologers, Chaldeans, and Soothsayers gathered before the 'writing on the wall,' and unable to read the characters or make known the interpretation. We have a right to rejoice when a true seer comes at last, some man in whom is an excellent spirit, to whom have been given light, wisdom, and understanding; who can accurately read the 'Mene, Mene, Tekel, Upharsin' of an original mind (however unripe, however inefficiently cultured and partially expanded that mind may be); and who can say with confidence, 'This is the interpretation thereof.

Yet even the writer to whom I allude shares the mistake about the authorship, and does me the injustice to suppose that there was equivoque in my former rejection of this honour (as an honour I regard it). May I assure him that I would scorn in this and in every other case to deal in equivoque; I believe language to have been given us to make our meaning clear, and not to wrap it in dishonest doubt?

'The Tenant of Wildfell Hall,' by Acton Bell, had likewise an unfavourable reception. At this I cannot wonder. The choice of subject was an entire mistake. Nothing less congruous with the writer's nature could be conceived. The motives which dictated this choice were pure, but, I think, slightly morbid. She had, in the course of her life, been called on to contemplate, near at hand, and for a long time, the terrible effects of talents misused and faculties abused: hers was naturally a sensitive, reserved, and dejected nature; what she saw sank very deeply into her mind; it did her harm. She brooded over it till she believed it to be a duty to reproduce every detail (of course with fictitious characters, incidents, and situations), as a warning to others. She hated her work, but would pursue it. When reasoned with on the subject, she regarded such reasonings as a temptation to self-indulgence. She must be honest; she must not varnish, soften, nor conceal. This well-meant resolution brought on her misconstruction, and some abuse, which she bore, as it was her custom to bear whatever was unpleasant, with mild, steady patience. She was a very sincere, and practical Christian, but the tinge of religious melancholy communicated a sad shade to her brief, blameless life.

Neither Ellis nor Acton allowed herself for one moment to sink under want of encouragement; energy nerved the one, and endurance upheld the other. They were both prepared to try again; I would fain think that hope and the sense of power were yet strong within them. But a great change approached; affliction came in that shape which to anticipate is dread; to look back on, grief. In the very heat and burden of the day, the labourers failed over their work.

My sister Emily first declined. The details of her illness are deep-branded in my memory, but to dwell on them, either in thought or narrative, is not in my power. Never in all her life had she lingered over any task that lay before her, and she did not linger now. She sank rapidly. She made haste to leave us. Yet, while physically she perished, mentally she grew stronger than we had yet known her. Day by day, when I saw with what a front she met suffering, I looked on her with an anguish of wonder and love. I have seen nothing like it; but, indeed, I have never seen her parallel in anything. Stronger than a man, simpler than a child, her nature stood alone. The awful point was, that while full of ruth for others, on herself she had no pity; the spirit was inexorable to the flesh; from the trembling hand, the unnerved limbs, the faded eyes, the same service was exacted as they had rendered in health. To stand by and witness this, and not dare to remonstrate, was a pain no words can render.

Two cruel months of hope and fear passed painfully by, and the day came at last when the terrors and pains of death were to be undergone by this treasure, which had grown dearer and dearer to our hearts as it wasted before our eyes. Towards the decline of that day, we had nothing of Emily but her mortal remains as consumption left them. She died December 19, 1848.

We thought this enough: but we were utterly and presumptuously wrong. She was not buried ere Anne fell ill. She had not been committed to the grave a fortnight, before we received distinct intimation that it was necessary to prepare our minds to see the younger sister go after the elder. Accordingly, she followed in the same path with slower step, and with a patience that equalled the other's fortitude. I have said that she was religious, and it was by leaning on those Christian doctrines in which she firmly believed, that she found support through her most painful journey. I witnessed their efficacy in her latest hour and greatest trial, and must bear my testimony to the calm triumph with which they brought her through. She died May 28, 1849.

What more shall I say about them? I cannot and need not say much more. In externals, they were two unobtrusive women; a perfectly secluded life gave them retiring manners and habits. In Emily's nature the extremes of vigour and simplicity seemed to meet. Under an unsophisticated culture, inartificial tastes, and an unpretending outside, lay a secret power and fire that might have informed the brain and kindled the veins of a hero; but she had no worldly wisdom; her powers were unadapted to the practical business of life; she would fail to defend her most manifest rights, to consult her most legitimate advantage. An interpreter ought always to have stood between her and the world. Her will was not very flexible, and it generally opposed her interest. Her temper was magnanimous, but warm and sudden; her spirit altogether unbending.

Anne's character was milder and more subdued; she wanted

the power, the fire, the originality of her sister, but was well endowed with quiet virtues of her own. Long-suffering, self-denying, reflective, and intelligent, a constitutional reserve and taciturnity placed and kept her in the shade, and covered her mind, and especially her feelings, with a sort of nun-like veil, which was rarely lifted. Neither Emily nor Anne was learned; they had no thought of filling their pitchers at the well-spring of other minds; they always wrote from the impulse of nature, the dictates of intuition, and from such stores of observation as their limited experience had enabled them to amass. I may sum up all by saying, that for strangers they were nothing, for superficial observers less than nothing; but for those who had known them all their lives in the intimacy of close relationship, they were genuinely good and truly great.

This notice has been written because I felt it a sacred duty to wipe the dust off their gravestones, and leave their dear names free from soil.

CURRER BELL

AN EXCERPT FROM
Charlotte Bronte's Notes on
the Pseudonyms Used, 1850

CHARLOTTE AND EMILY BRONTË

BY MILLICENT FAWCETT

In the quiet Yorkshire village of Haworth, on the bleak moorland hillside above Keighley, were born two of the greatest imaginative writers of the present century, Charlotte and Emily Brontë. The wonderful gifts of the Brontë family, the grief and tragedy that overshadowed their lives, and their early deaths, will always cast about their story a peculiarly touching interest. Their father, the Rev. Patrick Brontë, was of Irish birth. He was born in the County Down, of a Protestant family—one that had migrated from the south to the north of Ireland. His character was that which we are more accustomed to associate with Scotland than with Ireland. Resolute, stern, independent, and self-denying, he had the virtues of an old Covenanter rather than the facile graces which so often distinguish those of Celtic blood. His father was a farmer, but Patrick Brontë had no desire to live by agricultural industry. At sixteen years of age he separated himself from his family and opened a school. What amount of success he had in this undertaking does not appear, but it is evident that he had a distinct object in view, namely, to obtain money enough to complete his own education; in this he was successful, for after nine years' labour in instructing others, he entered as a student in St. John's College, Cambridge, remained there four years, obtained the B.A. degree of the University, and was ordained as a clergyman of the Church of England. He kept up no intercourse with his family, and showed no trace of his Irish blood, either in speech or character. He loved and married Miss Branwell, of

Penzance, a lady of much sweetness and refinement. Their six children were destined, through the writings of two of them, to be known wherever the English language is spoken, all over the world. After holding livings in Essex and at Thornton, in Yorkshire, Mr. Brontë was appointed to the Rectory of Haworth, which is now so often visited on account of its association with the authors of *Jane Eyre* and *Wuthering Heights*.

Mrs. Brontë's six children were born in rapid succession, and her naturally delicate constitution was further tried by the constant labour and anxiety involved in providing, on very limited means, for the wants of the little brood. Mrs. Gaskell, in her *Life of Charlotte Brontë*, appears to imply that, more than is even usually the case, the weight of family cares and anxieties fell upon the mother rather than the father. "Mr. Brontë," she says, "was, of course, much engaged in his study, and besides, he was not naturally fond of children, and felt their frequent appearance upon the scene as a drag both on his wife's strength and as an interruption to the comfort of the household." One feels disposed to comment on this by saying that children ought never to be born if either of their parents inclines to regard them "as an interruption to the comfort of the household." To give life and grudge it at the same time is not an attractive combination of qualities. Though not much helped by her husband, Mrs. Brontë was, however, not alone in her domestic cares and duties; the eldest of the "interruptions to the comfort of the household," Maria, was a child of wonderfully precocious intellect and heart. Her remarkable character was described in after years by her sister Charlotte as the Helen Burns of *Jane Eyre*. In her, her mother found a sympathising companion and a helper in her domestic cares. The time was rapidly approaching when the mother's place in the household would be vacant, and when many of its duties and responsibilities would be discharged by Maria.

The little Brontës were from their birth unlike other children. The room dedicated to their use was not, even in their babyhood, called their nursery; it was their "study." Little Maria at seven years old would shut herself up in this study with the newspaper, and be able to converse with her father on all the public events of the day, and instruct the other children as to current politics, and upon the characters of the chief personages of the political world.

Mrs. Brontë died in 1821. Maria was then eight; Elizabeth, seven; Charlotte, five; Patrick Branwell, four; Emily, three; and Anne, one. The little motherless brood were left alone for a year, when an elder sister of their mother came to live at the parsonage, but she does not seem to have had any real influence over them. She taught the girls to stitch and sew, and to become proficient in various domestic arts, but she had no sympathy or communion with them, and their real life was lived quite apart from hers. As soon almost as they could read and write at all, they began to compose plays and act them; they had no society but each other's; this, however, was all-sufficient for them. Their power of invention and imagination was very marked; to the habit of composing stories in their own minds they gave the name of "making out." As soon as the labour of writing became less formidable than it always is to baby fingers, the stories thus "made out" were written down. In fifteen months, when Charlotte was about twelve to thirteen years of age, she wrote twenty-two volumes of manuscript, in the minutest hand, which can hardly be deciphered except with the aid of a magnifying-glass. The Duke of Wellington filled a large place in the minds of the Brontës, and in their romances. Something of what the hero was to them when they were children, Charlotte afterwards put into the mouth of Shirley, the heroine of her novel of that name. After the manner of imaginative children, she not only worshipped her hero from afar, but identified herself with him or with members of his family. The authorship of many of her childish romances and poems is ascribed, in her imagination, to the Marquis of Douro, or Lord Charles Wellesley; and when these "goodly youths" are not introduced as authors they often become the chief personages of the story.

The shadow of death that casts so deep a gloom over the story of the Brontë family, first fell on Maria and Elizabeth, the two elder children. The four girls—Maria, Elizabeth, Charlotte, and Emily—had been sent to a school, which was partly a charitable institution, at Cowan Bridge, in Westmoreland. The living at Haworth parsonage was the reverse of luxurious, but the food and the sanitary arrangements at Cowan Bridge were so bad that the health of the little Brontës was seriously injured by it. The food was repulsive from the want of cleanliness with which it was prepared and placed on the table. The children frequently refused food altogether, though sinking from the want of it, rather than drink the "bingy" milk, and eat unappetising scraps from a dirty larder, and puddings made with water taken from rain-tubs and impregnated with the smell of soot and dust. Besides the faulty domestic arrangements of the school, the discipline was harsh and tyrannical, and one teacher in particular was guilty of conduct towards Maria Brontë that can only be called brutal. Low fever broke out at the school, from which about forty of the pupils suffered, but the Brontës did not take the disease. It was evident that Maria was destined for another fate, that of consumption. She was removed from the school only a few days before her death, and Elizabeth followed her to the grave about six weeks later, in June 1825. Even after this Mr. Brontë's eyes were not opened to the danger his children were in by their treatment at Cowan Bridge, and Charlotte and Emily were still allowed to remain at the school. It soon, however, became evident that they would not be long in following Maria and Elizabeth unless they were removed; and they returned home before the rigours of another winter set in. All the physical and mental tortures she endured at Cowan Bridge, Charlotte afterwards described in the account she gives of "Lowood" in *Jane Eyre*. It is not to be taken that the account of "Lowood" is as strictly an accurate description of Cowan Bridge as Charlotte Brontë would have given if she had been simply writing a history of the school. The facts are, perhaps, magnified by the lurid glow of passion and grief with which she recalled her sisters' sufferings. She was only between nine and ten when she left Cowan Bridge, and in the account she wrote of it twenty years later we see rather the impression that was left on her imagination than a strictly accurate history; but there is no doubt that in her account of Maria Brontë's angelic patience, and the cruel persecution to which she was subjected by one of the teachers, the Lowood of *Jane Eyre* is a perfectly faithful transcript of what took place at Cowan Bridge. Mrs. Gaskell says, "Not a word of that part of *Jane Eyre* but is a literal repetition of scenes between the pupil and the teacher. Those who had been pupils at the same time knew who must have written the book from the force with which Helen Burns's sufferings are described."

After the death of Maria and Elizabeth, the next great sorrow of the Brontë family arose from the career of the only son, Patrick Branwell. He was a handsome boy of exceptional mental powers. He had in particular the gift of brilliant conversation, and there was hardly anything he attempted in the way of talking, writing, or drawing which he did not do well. In one of Charlotte's letters she says, "You ask me if I do not think that men are strange beings? I do, indeed. I have often thought so; and I think, too, that the mode of bringing them up is strange; they are not sufficiently guarded from temptation. Girls are protected as if they were something very frail and silly indeed, while boys are turned loose on the world, as if they of all beings in existence were the wisest and least liable to be led astray." Poor Branwell, with his brilliant social qualities, was not sufficiently guarded from temptation. The easiest outlet from the narrow walls of Haworth parsonage was to be found at the little inn of Haworth village. The habit of the place was, when any stranger arrived at the inn, for the host to send for the brilliant boy from the parsonage to amuse the guest. The result will easily be guessed. The guiding principle of Charlotte's character was her inexorable fidelity to duty; her whole nature turned with irresistible force to what was right rather than to what was pleasant. With Branwell the reverse was the case.

Conventional propriety of course strictly guarded Charlotte from the possible dangers of associating with casual strangers at the village inn, although her strong resolute character would not have run a tenth part of the risk of contamination as did that of the weak, pleasure-seeking Branwell. It is needless to dwell on the details of his gradual degradation; the high ideals and hopes of his youth were given up; his character became at once coarse and weak. He was entirely incapable of self-government and of retaining any kind of respectable employment. His intemperance and other vices made the daily life of his sisters at the parsonage a nightmare of horrors. For eight years the young man, whose boyhood his family had watched with so much hope and pride, was a source of shame and anguish to them, all the more keenly felt because it could not be openly avowed. Many who knew the family affirmed that so far as purely intellectual qualities were concerned Branwell was even more eminently distinguished than his sisters; but mere intellect, without moral power to guide it, is as dangerous as a spirited horse without bit or bridle. Branwell was singularly deficient in that moral power in which his sisters were so strong, and his education did nothing to supply this natural deficiency. He died in 1848, at the age of thirty.

Cowan Bridge was not the only experience Charlotte and Emily had of school life. They went for a time to another school at Roe Head, where Charlotte was very happy, and in 1835 she returned to the same school as a teacher. In 1842 Charlotte and Emily went to a school in Brussels, where the former stayed two years, the latter only one. All that Charlotte saw and all the friends she made were afterwards portrayed in her stories. One of her most intimate friends became the Caroline Helstone of *Shirley*; the originals of Rose and Jessie Yorke were also among her schoolfellows at Roe Head. There can be little doubt that M. Paul Emanuel of Villette was M. Héger of the Brussels school. Every trivial circumstance of an unusually uneventful life became food for her imagination.

The development of Emily's genius was different. Her love of the moors around Haworth was so intense that it was impossible for her to thrive when she was away from them. It became a fact recognised by all the family that Emily must not be taken away from home. The solitude of the wild, dark moors, and the communing with her own heart, together with the dark tragedy of Branwell's wasted life, were the sole sources of Emily's inspiration. Her poems have a wild, untameable quality in them, and her one romance, *Wuthering Heights*, places her in the first rank among the great imaginative writers of English fiction. There is something terrible in Emily's sternness of character, which she never vented pitilessly on any one but herself. She was deeply reserved, and hardly ever, even to her sisters, spoke of what she felt most intensely. A friend who furnished Mrs. Gaskell with some particulars for her biography, states that on one occasion she mentioned "that some one had asked me what religion I was of (with the view of getting me for a partisan), and that I had said that was between God and me. Emily, who was lying on the hearth-rug, exclaimed, 'That's right.' This was all," adds the friend, "I ever heard Emily say on religious subjects." Emily's love for animals was intense; she was especially devoted to a savage old bull-dog named Keeper, who owned no master but herself. The incident in *Shirley* of the heroine being bitten by a mad dog, and straightway burning the wound herself with a red-hot Italian iron, was true of Emily. Her last illness was a time of terrible agony to Charlotte and Anne, not merely because they saw that she who, Charlotte said, was the thing that seemed nearest to her heart in the world was going to be taken from them, but because Emily's resistance to the inroads of illness was so terrible. She resolutely refused to see a doctor, and she would allow no nursing and no tender helpfulness of any kind. It was evident to her agonised sisters that she was dying, but she maintained her savage reserve, suffering in solitary silence rather than admit her pain and weakness. On the very day of her death she rose as usual, dressed herself, and attempted to carry on her usual employments, and all this with the catching, rattling breath and the glazing eye which told that the hand of Death was actually upon her. Charlotte wrote in this agonising hour, "Moments so dark as these I have never known. I pray for God's support to us all. Hitherto He has granted it." At noon on that day, when it was too late, Emily whispered in gasps, "If you will send for a doctor, I will see him now." A few days later Charlotte wrote, "We are very calm at present. Why should we be otherwise? The anguish of seeing her suffer is over; the spectacle of the pains of death is gone by; the funeral day is past. We feel she is at peace. No need to tremble for the hard frost and the keen wind. Emily does not feel them." The terrible anguish of those last days haunted the surviving sisters like a vision of doom. Nearly six months later Charlotte wrote again that nothing but hope in the life to come had kept her heart from breaking. "I cannot forget," she says, "Emily's death-day; it becomes a more fixed, a darker, a more frequently recurring idea in my mind than ever. It was very terrible. She was torn, conscious, panting, reluctant, though resolute, out of a happy life." Within a very short time the gentle youngest sister Anne also died, and Charlotte was left with her father, the last survivor of the family of six wonderful children who had come to Haworth twenty-nine years before.

In earlier and happier days the habit of the sisters had been, when their aunt went to bed at nine o'clock, to put out the candles and pace up and down the room discussing the plots of their novels, and making plans and projects for their future life. Now Charlotte was left to pace the room alone, with all that had been dearest to her in the world under the church pavement at Haworth and in the old churchyard at Scarborough. But Charlotte was not one to give way to self-indulgent idleness, even in the hour of darkest despair. She was writing *Shirley* at the time of Anne's last illness. After the death of this beloved and only remaining sister, she resumed her task; but those who knew what her private history at the time was, can trace in the pages of the novel what she had gone through. The first chapter she wrote after the death of Anne is called, "The Valley of the Shadow of Death."

The first venture in authorship of the sisters was a volume of poems, to which they each contributed. They imagined, probably with justice, that the world was at that time prejudiced against literary women. Therefore they were careful to conceal, even from their publishers, their real identity. The poems were published as the writings of Currer, Ellis, and Acton Bell.

Jane Eyre was the first of Charlotte's stories which was published, but *The Professor* was the first that was written with a view to publication. The sisters each wrote a story—Charlotte, *The Professor*; Emily, *Wuthering Heights*; and Anne, *Agnes Grey*, and sent them to various publishers. Charlotte was the only one of the three sisters whose manuscript was returned on her hands. But she was not discouraged by the disappointment. Just at this time Mr. Brontë, who had been suffering from cataract, was persuaded by his daughters to go to Manchester for an operation. Charlotte accompanied him, and it was while she was waiting on him, in the long suspense after the operation had been performed, that she began *Jane Eyre*, the book that made her, and ultimately the name of Brontë, famous. Nothing is more striking in Charlotte's personal history than the way in which she reproduced the events and personages of her own circle into her novels. Probably the belief that she was writing anonymously encouraged her in this. Her father's threatened blindness and her own fear of a similar calamity are reflected, as it were, in the blindness of Rochester in *Jane Eyre*. The success of *Jane Eyre* was rapid and complete, and there was much dispute whether its author were a man or a woman. The *Quarterly Review* distinguished itself by the remark that if the author were a woman it was evident "she must be one who for some sufficient reason has long forfeited the society of her sex." Sensitive as Charlotte Brontë was, the coarseness of the insult could not wound her; it could at the utmost be regarded as nothing worse than a trivial annoyance; for when the words reached Charlotte, the grave had not long closed over Branwell's wasted life; Emily was just dead, and it was evident that Anne was dying. The greatness of her grief and the anguish of her loneliness dwarfed to their proper proportions the petty insults that at another time would have caused her acute pain. On the whole she had nothing to complain of in the way her book was received; she suffered no lack of generous appreciation from the real leaders of the literary world. Thackeray and G. H. Lewes, Miss Martineau, and Sidney Dobell were warm in their praise of her work. Charlotte's manner of making her literary fame known to her father was characteristic. The secret of their authorship had been very strictly kept by the sisters; but when the success of *Jane Eyre* was assured, Emily and Anne urged Charlotte that their father ought to be allowed to share the pleasure of knowing that she was the writer of the book. Accordingly one afternoon Charlotte entered her father's study and said, "Papa, I've been writing a book." When Mr. Brontë found that the book was not only written, but printed and published, he exclaimed, "My dear, you've never thought of the expense it will be! It will be almost sure to be a loss, for how can you get a book sold? No one knows you or your name."

"But, papa, I don't think it will be a loss; no more will you, if you will just let me read you a review or two, and tell you more about it." At tea that evening Mr. Brontë exclaimed to his other daughters, "Girls, do you know that Charlotte has been writing a book, and it is much better than likely?"

The pacing up and down of the sisters in the firelight, discussing the plots of their novels, has been already mentioned. Mrs. Gaskell records that Charlotte told her that these discussions seldom had any effect in causing her to change the events in her stories, "so possessed was she with the feeling that she had described reality." This confirms what Mr. Swinburne has said of her strongest characteristic as an author, that she has the power of making the reader feel in every nerve that thus and not otherwise it must have been. It must not, however, be thought that the conversations with her sisters were therefore useless; no doubt they were very stimulating to her imagination, and gave her creations more solid reality than they would otherwise have had.

In 1854 Charlotte Brontë married Mr. Nicholls, an Irish gentleman, who had for eight years been her father's curate. She only lived nine months after her marriage. She was happy in her husband's love, and appreciated his devotion to his parish duties. But the loving admirers of Charlotte Brontë can never feel much enthusiasm for Mr. Nicholls. Mrs. Gaskell states that he was not attracted by her literary fame, but was rather repelled by it; he appears to have used her up remorselessly, in their short married life, in the routine drudgery of parish work. She did not complain; on the contrary, she seemed more than contented to sacrifice everything for him and his work; but she remarks in one of her letters, "I have less time for thinking." Apparently she had none for writing. Surely the husband of a Charlotte Brontë, just as much as the wife of a Wordsworth or a Tennyson, ought to be attracted by literary fame. To be the life partner of one to whom the most precious of Nature's gifts is confided, and to be unappreciative of it and even repelled by it, shows a littleness of nature and essential meanness of soul. A true wife or husband of one of these gifted beings should rather regard herself or himself as responsible to the world for making the conditions of the daily life of their distinguished partners favourable to the development of their genius. But pearls have before now been cast before swine, and one cannot but regret that Charlotte Brontë was married to a man who did not value her place in literature as he ought.

AN EXCERPT FROM
Some Eminent Women of our Times
- Short Biographical Sketches, 1889

THE SISTERS BRONTË

BY MRS. OLIPHANT

The effect produced upon the general mind by the appearance of Charlotte Brontë in literature, and afterwards by the record of her life when that was over, is one which it is nowadays somewhat difficult to understand. Had the age been deficient in the art of fiction, or had it followed any long level of mediocrity in that art, we could have comprehended this more easily. But Charlotte Brontë appeared in the full flush of a period more richly endowed than any other we know of in that special branch of literature, so richly endowed, indeed, that the novel had taken quite fictitious importance, and the names of Dickens and Thackeray ranked almost higher than those of any living writers except perhaps Tennyson, then young and on his promotion too. Anthony Trollope and Charles Reade who, though in their day extremely popular, have never had justice from a public which now seems almost to have forgotten them, formed a powerful second rank to these two great names. It is a great addition to the value of the distinction gained by the new comer that it was acquired in an age so rich in the qualities of the imagination.

But this only increases the wonder of a triumph which had no artificial means to heighten it, nothing but genius on the part of a writer possessing little experience or knowledge of the world, and no sort of social training or adventitious aid. The genius was indeed unmistakable, and possessed in a very high degree the power of expressing itself in the most vivid and actual pictures of life. But the life of which it had command was seldom attractive, often narrow, local, and of a kind which meant keen personal satire more than any broader view of human existence. A group of commonplace clergymen, intense against their little parochial background as only the most real art of portraiture, intensified by individual scorn and dislike, could have made them: the circle of limited interests, small emulations, keen little spites and rancours, filling the atmosphere of a great boarding school, the Brussels *Pensionnat des filles*—these were the two spheres chiefly portrayed: but portrayed with an absolute untempered force which knew neither charity, softness, nor even impartiality, but burned upon the paper and made everything round dim in the contrast. I imagine it was this extraordinary naked force which was the great cause of a success, never perhaps like the numerical successes in literature of the present day, when edition follows edition, and thousand thousand, of the books which are the favourites of the public: but one which has lived and lasted through nearly half a century, and is even now potent enough to carry on a little literature of its own, book after book following each other not so much to justify as to reproclaim and echo to all the winds the fame originally won. No one else of the century, I think, has called forth this persevering and lasting homage. Not Dickens, though perhaps more of him than of any one else has been dealt out at intervals to an admiring public; not Thackeray, of whom still we know but little; not George Eliot, though her fame has more solid foundations than that of Miss Brontë. Scarcely Scott has called forth more continual droppings of elucidation, explanation, remark. Yet the books upon which this tremendous reputation is founded though vivid, original, and striking in the highest degree, are not great books. Their philosophy of life is that of a schoolgirl, their knowledge of the world almost *nil*, their conclusions confused by the haste and passion of a mind self-centred and working in the narrowest orbit. It is rather, as we have said, the most incisive and realistic art of portraiture than any exercise of the nobler arts of fiction—imagination, combination, construction—or humorous survey of life or deep apprehension of its problems—upon which this fame is built.

The curious circumstance that Charlotte Brontë was, if the word may be so used, doubled by her sisters, the elder, Emily, whose genius has been taken for granted, carrying the wilder elements of the common inspiration to extremity in the strange, chaotic and weird romance of "Wuthering Heights," while Anne diluted such powers of social observation as were in the family into two mildly disagreeable novels of a much commoner order, has no doubt also enhanced the central figure of the group to an amazing degree. They placed her strength in relief by displaying its separate elements, and thus commending the higher skill and larger spirit which took in both, understanding the moors and wild country and rude image of man better than the one, and misunderstanding the common course of more subdued life less than the other. The three together are for ever inseparable; they were homely, lowly, somewhat neglected in their lives, had few opportunities and few charms to the careless eye: yet no group of women, undistinguished by rank, unendowed by beauty, and known to but a limited circle of friends as unimportant as themselves have ever, I think, in the course of history—certainly never in this century—come to such universal recognition. The effect is quite unique, unprecedented, and difficult to account for; but there cannot be the least doubt that it is a matter of absolute fact which nobody can deny.

* * * * *

These three daughters of a poor country clergyman came into the world early in the century, the dates of their births being 1816, 1818, 1820, in the barest of little parsonages in the midst of the moors—a wild but beautiful country, and a rough but highly characteristic and keen-witted people. Yorkshire is the very heart of England; its native force, its keen practical sense, its rough wit, and the unfailing importance in the nation of the largest of the shires has given it a strong individual character and position almost like that of an independent province. But the Brontës, whose name is a softened and decorated edition of a common Irish name, were not of that forcible race: and perhaps the strong strain after emotion, and revolt against the monotonies of life, which were so conspicuous in them were more easily traceable to their Celtic origin than many other developments attributed to that cause. They were motherless from an early age, children of a father who, after having been depicted as a capricious tyrant, seems now to have found a fairer representation as a man with a high spirit and peculiar temper, yet neither unkind to his family nor uninterested in their welfare. There was one son, once supposed to be the hero and victim of a disagreeable romance, but apparent now as only a specimen, not alas, uncommon, of the ordinary ne'er-do-well of a family, without force of character or self-control to keep his place with decency in the world.

These children all scribbled from their infancy as soon as the power of inscribing words upon paper was acquired by them, inventing imaginary countries and compiling visionary records of them as so many imaginative children do. The elder girl and boy made one pair, the younger girls another, connected by the closest links of companionship. It was thought or hoped that the son was the genius of the family, and at the earliest possible age he began to send his effusions to editors, and to seek admission to magazines with the mingled arrogance and humility of a half-fledged creature. But the world knows now that it was not poor Branwell who was the genius of the family; and this injury done him in his cradle, and the evil report of him that everybody gives throughout his life, awakens a certain pity in the mind for the unfortunate youth so unable to keep any supremacy among the girls whom he must have considered his natural inferiors and vassals. We are told by Charlotte Brontë herself that he never knew of the successes of his sisters, the fact of their successive publications being concealed from him out of tenderness for his feelings; but it is scarcely to be credited that when the parish knew the unfortunate brother did not find out. The unhappy attempt of Mrs. Gaskell in writing the lives of the sisters to make this melancholy young man accountable for the almost brutal element in Emily Brontë's conception of life, and the strange views of Charlotte as to what men were capable of, has made him far too important in their history; where, indeed, he had no need to have appeared at all, had the family pride consisted, as the pride of so many families does, in veiling rather than exhibiting the faults of its members. So far as can be made out now, he had as little as possible to do with their development in any way.

There was nothing unnatural or out of the common in the youthful life of the family except that strange gift of genius, which though consistent with every genial quality of being, in such a nature as that of Scott, seems in other developments of character to turn all the elements into chaos. Its effect upon the parson's three daughters was, indeed, not of a very wholesome kind. It awakened in them an uneasy sense of superiority which gave double force to every one of the little hardships which a girl in a great school of a charitable kind, and a governess in a middle-class house, has to support: and made life harder instead of sweeter to them in many ways, since it was full of the biting experience of conditions less favourable than those of many persons round them whom they could not but feel inferior to themselves.

The great school, which it was Charlotte Brontë's first act when she began her literary career to invest with an almost tragic character of misery, privation, and wrong, was her first step from home. Yorkshire schools did not at that period enjoy a very good reputation in the world, and Nicholas Nickleby was forming his acquaintance with the squalid cruelty of Dotheboys Hall just about the same time when Charlotte Brontë's mind was being filled with the privations and discontents of Lowood. In such a case there is generally some fire where there is so much smoke, and probably Lowood was under no very heavenly *régime*: but at the same time its drawbacks were sharply accentuated by that keen criticism which is suggested by the constant sense of injured worth and consciousness of a superiority not acknowledged. The same feeling pursued her into the situations as governess which she occupied one after another, and in which her indignation at being expected to feel affection for the children put under her charge, forms a curious addition to the other grievances with which fate pursues her life. No doubt there are many temptations in the life of a governess; the position of a silent observer in a household, looking on at all its mistakes, and seeing the imperfection of its management with double force because of the effect they have on herself—especially if she feels herself competent, had she but the power, to set things right—must always be a difficult one. It was not continued long enough, however, to involve very much suffering; though no doubt it helped to mature the habit of sharp personal criticism and war with the world.

At the same time Charlotte Brontë made some very warm personal friendships, and wrote a great many letters to the school friends who pleased her, in which a somewhat stilted tone and demure seriousness is occasionally invaded by the usual chatter of girlhood, to the great improvement of the atmosphere if not of the mind. Ellen Nussey, Mary Taylor, women not manifestly intellectual but sensible and independent without either exaggeration of sentiment or hint of tragic story, remained her close friends as long as she lived, and her letters to them, though always a little demure, give us a gentler idea of her than anything else she has written. Not that there is much charm either of style or subject in them: but there is no sort of bitterness or sense of insufficient appreciation. Nothing can be more usual and commonplace, indeed, than this portion of her life. As in so many cases, the artificial lights thrown upon it by theories formed afterwards, clear away when we examine its actual records, and it is apparent that there was neither exceptional harshness of circumstance nor internal struggle in the existence of the girl who, though more or less in arms against everybody outside—especially when holding a position superior to her own, more especially still when exercising authority over her in any way—was yet quite an easy-minded, not unhappy, young woman at home, with friends to whom she could pour out long pages of what is, on the whole, quite moderate and temperate criticism of life, not without cheerful allusion to now and then a chance curate or other young person of the opposite sex, suspected of "paying attention" to one or other of the little coterie. These allusions are not more lofty or dignified than are similar notes of girls of less exalted pretensions, but there is not a touch in them of the keen pointed pen which afterwards put up the Haworth curates in all their imperfections before the world.

The other sisters at this time in the background, two figures always clinging together, looking almost like one, have no great share in this softer part of Charlotte's life. They were, though so different in character, completely devoted to each other, apparently forming no other friendships, each content with the one other partaker of her every thought. A little literature seems to have been created between them, little chapters of recollection and commentary upon their life, sealed up and put away for three years in each case, to be opened on Emily's or on Anne's birthday alternately, as a pathetic sign of their close unity, though the little papers were in themselves simple in the extreme. Anne too became a governess with something of the same experience as Charlotte, and uttering very hard judgments of unconscious people who were not the least unkind to her. But Emily had no such trials. She remained at home perhaps because she was too uncompromising to be allowed to make the experiment of putting up with other people, perhaps because one daughter at home was indispensable. The family seems to have had kind and trusted old servants, so that the cares of housekeeping did not weigh heavily upon the daughter in charge, and there is no evidence of exceptional hardness or roughness in their circumstances in any way.

In 1842, Charlotte and Emily, aged respectively twenty-six and twenty-four, went to Brussels. Their design was "to acquire a thorough familiarity with French," also some insight into other languages, with the view of setting up a school on their own account. The means were supplied by the aunt, who had lived in their house and taken more or less care of them since their mother's death. The two sisters were nearly a year in the Pensionnat Héger, now so perfectly known in every detail of its existence to all who have read "Villette." They were recalled by the death of the kind aunt who had procured them this advantage, and afterwards Charlotte, no one quite knows why, went back to Brussels for a second year, in which all her impressions were probably strengthened and intensified. Certainly a more clear and lifelike picture, scathing in its cold yet fierce light, was never made than that of the white tall Brussels house, its class rooms, its gardens, its hum of unamiable girls, its sharp display of rancorous and shrill teachers, its one inimitable professor. It startles the reader to find—a fact which we had forgotten— that M. Paul Emmanuel was M. Héger, the husband of Madame Héger and legitimate head of the house: and that this daring and extraordinary girl did not hesitate to encounter gossip or slander by making him so completely the hero of her romance. Slander in its commonplace form had nothing to do with such a fiery spirit as that of Charlotte Brontë: but it shows her perfect independence of mind and scorn of comment that she should have done this. In the end of '43 she returned home, and the episode was over. It was really the only episode of possible practical significance in her life until we come to the records of her brief literary career and her marriage, both towards its end.

* * * * *

The prospect of the school which the three sisters were to set up together was abandoned; there was no more talk of governessing. We are not told if it was the small inheritance of the aunt—only, Mr. Clement Shorter informs us, £1500—which enabled the sisters henceforward to remain at home without thought of further effort: but certainly this was what happened. And the lives of the two younger were drawing so near the end that it is a comfort to think that they enjoyed this moment of comparative grace together. Their life was extremely silent, secluded, and apart. There was the melancholy figure of Branwell to distract the house with the spectacle of heavy idleness, drink, and disorder; but this can scarcely have been so great an affliction as if he had been a more beloved brother. He was not, however, veiled by any tender attempt to cover his follies or wickedness, but openly complained of to all their friends, which mitigates the affliction: and they seem to have kept very separate from him, living in a world of their own.

In 1846 a volume of poems by Currer, Ellis, and Acton Bell, was published at their own cost. It had not the faintest success; they were informed by the publisher that two copies only had been sold, and the only satisfaction that remained to them was to send a few copies to some of the owners of those great names which the enthusiastic young women had worshipped from afar as stars in the firmament. These poems were re-published after Charlotte Brontë had attained her first triumph, and people had begun to cry out and wonder over "Wuthering Heights." The history of "Jane Eyre," on the other hand, is that of most works which have been the beginning of a career. It fell into the hands of the right man, the "reader" of Messrs. Smith, Elder and Co., Mr. Williams, a man of great intelligence and literary insight. The first story written by Charlotte Brontë, which was called "The Professor," and was the original of "Villette," written at a time when her mind was very full of the emotions raised by that singular portion of her life, had been rejected by a number of publishers, and was also rejected by Mr. Williams, who found it at once too crude and too *short* for the risks of publication, three volumes at that period being your only possible form for fiction. But he saw the power in it, and begged the author to try again at greater length. She did so; not on the basis of the "Professor" as might have seemed natural—probably the materials were still too much at fever-heat in her mind to be returned to at that moment—but by the story of "Jane Eyre," which at once placed Charlotte Brontë amid the most popular and powerful writers of her time.

I remember well the extraordinary thrill of interest which in the midst of all the Mrs. Gores, Mrs. Marshs, &c.—the latter name is mentioned along with those of Thackeray and Dickens even by Mr. Williams—came upon the reader who, in the calm of ignorance, took up the first volume of "Jane Eyre." The period of the heroine in white muslin, the immaculate creature who was of sweetness and goodness all compact, had lasted in the common lines of fiction up to that time. Miss Austen indeed might well have put an end to that abstract and empty fiction, yet it continued, as it always does continue more or less, the primitive ideal. But "Jane Eyre" gave her, for the moment, the *coup de grace*. That the book should be the story of a governess was perhaps necessary to the circumstances of the writer: and the governess was already a favourite figure in fiction. But generally she was of the beautiful, universally fascinating, all-enduring kind, the amiable blameless creature whose secret merits were never so hidden but that they might be perceived by a keen sighted hero. I am not sure, indeed, that anybody believed Miss Brontë when she said her heroine was plain. It is very clear from the story that Jane was never unnoticed, never failed to please, except among the women, whom it is the instinctive art of the novelist to rouse in arms against the central figure, thus demonstrating the jealousy, spite, and rancour native to their minds in respect to the women who please men. No male cynic was ever stronger on that subject than this typical woman. She cannot have believed it, I presume, since her closest friends were women, and she seems to have had perfect faith in their kindness: but this is a matter of conventional belief which has nothing to do with individual experience. It is one of the doctrines unassailable of the art of fiction; a thirty-ninth article in which every writer of novels is bound to believe.

Miss Brontë did not know fine ladies, and therefore, in spite of herself and a mind the reverse of vulgar, she made the competitors for Mr. Rochester's favour rather brutal and essentially vulgar persons, an error, curiously enough, which seems to have been followed by George Eliot in the corresponding scenes in "Mr. Gilfil's Love Story," where Captain Wybrow's *fiancée* treats poor Tiny very much as the beauty in Mr. Rochester's house treats Jane Eyre. Both were imaginary pictures, which perhaps more or less excuses their untruthfulness in writers both so sincere and lifelike in treating things they knew. It is amusing to remember that Jane Eyre's ignorance of dress gave a clinching argument to Miss Rigby in the *Quarterly* to decide that the writer was not and could not possibly be a woman. The much larger and more significant fact that no man (until in quite recent days when there have been instances of such effeminate art) ever made a woman so entirely the subject and inspiration of his book, the only interest in it, was entirely overlooked in what was, notwithstanding, the very shrewd and telling argument about the dress.

The chief thing, however, that distressed the candid and as yet unaccustomed reader in "Jane Eyre," and made him hope that it might be a man who had written it, was the character of Rochester's confidences to the girl whom he loved—not the character of Rochester, which was completely a woman's view, but that he should have talked to a girl so evidently innocent of his amours and his mistresses. This, however, I think, though, as we should have thought, a subject so abhorrent to a young woman such as Charlotte Brontë was, was also emphatically a woman's view. A man might have credited another man of Rochester's kind with impulses practically more heinous and designs of the worst kind: but he would not have made him err in that way.

In this was a point of honour which the woman did not understand. It marks a curious and subtle difference between the sexes. The woman less enlightened in practical evil considers less the risks of actual vice; but her imagination is free in other ways, and she innocently permits her hero to do and say things so completely against the code which is binding on gentlemen whether vicious or otherwise that her want of perception becomes conspicuous. The fact that the writer of the review in the *Quarterly* was herself a woman accounts for her mistake in supposing that the book was written if not by a man, by "a woman unsexed;" "a woman who had forfeited the society of her sex." And afterwards, when Mrs. Gaskell made her disastrous statements about Branwell Brontë and other associates of Charlotte's youth, it was with the hope of proving that the speech and manners of the men to whom she had been accustomed were of a nature to justify her in any such misapprehension of the usual manners of gentlemen. It was on the contrary, as I think, only the bold and unfettered imagination of a woman quite ignorant on all such subjects which could have suggested this special error. The mind of such a woman, casting about for something to make her wicked but delightful hero do by way of demonstrating his wickedness, yet preserving the fascination which she meant him to retain, probably hit upon this as the very wickedest thing she could think of, yet still attractive: for is there not a thrill of curiosity in searching out what such a strange being might think or say, which is of itself a strong sensation? Miss Brontë was, I think, the first to give utterance to that curiosity of the woman in respect to the man, and fascination of interest in him—not the ideal man, not Sir Kenneth, too reverent for anything but silent worship—which has since risen to such heights of speculation, and imprints now a tone upon modern fiction at which probably she would have been horrified.

* * * * *

There were numberless stories in those days of guilty love and betrayal, of how "lovely woman stoops to folly," and all the varieties of that endless subject; but it was, except in the comic vein, or with grotesque treatment, the pursuit of the woman by the man, the desire of the lover for the beloved which was the aim of fiction. A true lady of romance walked superior: she accepted (or not) the devotion: she stooped from her white height to reward her adorer: but that she herself should condescend to seek him (except under the circumstances of fashionable life, where everybody is in quest of a coronet), or call out for him to heaven and earth when he tarried in his coming, was unknown to the situations of romantic art. When the second of Charlotte Brontë's books appeared, there was accordingly quite a new sensation in store for the public. The young women in "Shirley" were all wild for this lover who, though promised by all the laws of nature and romance, did not appear. They leaned out of their windows, they stretched forth their hands, calling for him—appealing to heaven and earth. Why were they left to wear out their bloom, to lose their freshness, to spend their days in sewing and dreaming, when he, it was certain, was about somewhere, and by sheer perversity of fate could not find the way to them? Nothing was thought of the extra half-million of women in those days; perhaps it had not begun to exist; but that "nobody was coming to marry us, nobody coming to woo" was apparent.

Young ladies like Miss Charlotte Brontë and Miss Ellen Nussey her friend, would have died rather than give vent to such sentiments; but when the one of them to whom that gift was given found that her pen had become a powerful instrument in her hand, the current of the restrained feeling burst all boundaries, and she poured forth the cry which nobody had suspected before. It had been a thing to be denied, to be indignantly contradicted as impossible, if ever a lovesick girl put herself forth to the shame of her fellows and the laugh of the world. When such a phenomenon appeared, she was condemned as either bad or foolish by every law: and the idea that she was capable of "running after" a man was the most dreadful accusation that could be brought against a woman. Miss Brontë's heroines, however, did not precisely do this. Shirley and Caroline Helstone were not in love so much as longing for love, clamouring for it, feeling it to be their right of which they were somehow defrauded. There is a good deal to be said for such a view. If it is the most virtuous thing in the world for a man to desire to marry, to found a family, to be the father of children, it should be no shameful thing for a woman to own the same desire. But it is somehow against the instinct of primitive humanity, which has decided that the woman should be no more than responsive, maintaining a reserve in respect to her feelings, subduing the expression, unless in the "once, and only once, and to One only" of the poet.

Charlotte Brontë was the first to overthrow this superstition. Personally I am disposed to stand for the superstition, and dislike all transgression of it. But that was not the view of the most reticent and self-controlled of maidens, the little governess, clad in all the strict proprieties of the period, the parson's daughter despising curates, and unacquainted with other men. In her secret heart, she demanded of fate night and day why she, so full of life and capability, should be left there to dry up and wither; and why Providence refused her the completion of her being. Her heart was not set on a special love; still less was there anything fleshly or sensual in her imagination. It is a shame to use such words in speaking of her, even though to cast them forth as wholly inapplicable. The woman's grievance—that she should be left there unwooed, unloved, out of reach of the natural openings of life: without hope of motherhood: with the great instinct of her being unfulfilled—was almost a philosophical, and entirely an abstract, grievance, felt by her for her kind: for every woman dropped out of sight and unable to attain the manner of existence for which she was created. And I think it was the first time this cry had been heard out of the mouth of a perfectly modest and pure-minded woman, nay, out of the mouth of any woman; for it had nothing to do with the shriek of the Sapphos for love. It was more startling, more confusing to the general mind, than the wail of the lovelorn. The gentle victim of "a disappointment," or even the soured and angered victim, was a thing quite understood and familiar: but not the woman calling upon heaven and earth to witness that all the fates were conspiring against her to cheat her of her natural career.

So far as I can see this was the great point which gave force to Charlotte Brontë's genius and conferred upon her the curious pre-eminence she possesses among the romancers of her time. In this view "Shirley," though I suppose the least popular, is the most characteristic of her works. It is dominated throughout with this complaint. Curates? Yes, there they are, a group of them. Is that the thing you expect us women to marry? Yet it is our right to bear children, to guide the house. And we are half of the world, and where is the provision for us?

This cry disturbed the critic, the reader, the general public in the most curious way; they did not know what to make of it. Was it a shameless woman who was so crying out? It is always the easiest way, and one which avoids all complications, to say so, and thus crush every question. But it was scarcely easy to believe this in face of other circumstances. Mrs. Gaskell, as much puzzled as any one, when Charlotte Brontë's short life was over, tried hard to account for it by "environment" as the superior persons say, that is by the wicked folly of her brother, and the coarseness of all the Yorkshiremen round; and thus originated in her bewilderment, let us hope without other intention, a new kind of biography, as the subject of it inaugurated an entirely new kind of social revolution. The cry of the women indeed almost distressed as well as puzzled the world. The vivid genius still held it, but the ideas were alarming, distracting beyond measure. The *Times* blew a trumpet of dismay; the book was revolution as well as revelation. It was an outrage upon good taste, it was a betrayal of sentiments too widespread to be comfortable. It was indelicate if not immodest. We have outgrown now the very use of this word, but it was a potent one at that period. And it was quite a just reproach. That cry shattered indeed altogether the "delicacy" which was supposed to be the most exquisite characteristic of womankind. The softening veil is blown away, when such exhibitions of feeling are given to the world.

From that period to this is a long step. We have travelled

through many years and many gradations of sentiment: and we have now arrived at a standard of opinion by which the "sex-problem" has become the most interesting of questions, the chief occupation of fiction, to be discussed by men and women alike with growing warmth and openness, the immodest and the indelicate being equally and scornfully dismissed as barriers with which Art has nothing to do. My impression is that Charlotte Brontë was the pioneer and founder of this school of romance, though it would probably have shocked and distressed her as much as any other woman of her age.

* * * * *

The novels of Emily and Anne Brontë were published shortly after "Jane Eyre," in three volumes, of which "Wuthering Heights" occupied the first two. I am obliged to confess that I have never shared the common sentiment of enthusiasm for that, to me, unlovely book. The absence of almost every element of sympathy in it, the brutality and misery, tempered only by an occasional gleam of the heather, the freshness of an occasional blast over the moors, have prevented me from appreciating a force which I do not deny but cannot admire. The figure of Heathcliffe, which perhaps has called forth more praise than any other single figure in the literature of the time, does not touch me. I can understand how in the jumble which the reader unconsciously makes, explaining him more or less by Rochester and other of Charlotte Brontë's heroes, he may take his place in a sort of system, and thus have humanities read into him, so to speak, which he does not himself possess. But though the horror and isolation of the house is powerful I have never been able to reconcile myself either to the story or treatment, or to the estimate of Emily Brontë's genius held so strongly by so many people. There is perhaps the less harm in refraining from much comment on this singular book, of which I gladly admit the unique character, since it has been the occasion of so many and such enthusiastic comments. To me Emily Brontë is chiefly interesting as the double of her sister, exaggerating at once and softening her character and genius as showing those limits of superior sense and judgment which restrained her, and the softer lights which a better developed humanity threw over the landscape common to them both. We perceive better the tempering sense of possibility by which Charlotte made her rude and almost brutal hero still attractive, even in his masterful ferocity, when we see Emily's incapacity to express anything in *her* hero except perhaps a touch of that tragic pathos, prompting to fiercer harshness still, which is in the soul of a man who never more, whatever he does, can set himself right. This is the one strain of poetry to my mind in the wild conception. There was no measure in the younger sister's thoughts, nor temperance in her methods.

The youngest of all, the gentle Anne, would have no right to be considered at all as a writer but for her association with these imperative spirits. An ordinary little novelette and a moral story, working out the disastrous knowledge gained by acquaintance with the unfortunate Branwell's ruinous habits, were her sole productions. She was the element wanting in Emily's rugged work and nature. Instead of being two sisters constantly entwined with each other, never separate when they could help it, had Anne been by some fantastic power swamped altogether and amalgamated with her best beloved, we may believe that Emily might then have shown herself the foremost of the three. But the group as it stands is more interesting than any single individual could be. And had Charlotte Brontë lived a long and triumphant life, a fanciful writer might have imagined that the throwing off of those other threads of being so closely attached to her own had poured greater force and charity into her veins. But we are baffled in all our suggestions for the amendment of the ways of Providence.

*　*　*　*　*

The melancholy and tragic year, or rather six months, which swept from Haworth Parsonage three of its inmates, and left Charlotte and her father alone to face life as they might, was now approaching; and it seems so completely an episode in the story of the elder sister's genius as well as her life, that its history is like that of an unwritten tragedy, hers as much as her actual work. Branwell was the first to die, unwept yet not without leaving a pathetic note in the record. Then came the extraordinary passion and agony of Emily, which has affected the imagination so much, and which, had it been for any noble purpose, would have been a true martyrdom. But to die the death of a Stoic, in fierce resistance yet subjection to Nature, regardless of the feelings of all around, for the sake of pride and self-will alone, is not an act to be looked upon with the reverential sympathy which, however, it has secured from many. The strange creature with her shoes on her feet and her staff in her hand, refusing till the last to acknowledge herself to be ill or to receive any help in her weakness, gives thus a kind of climax to her strange and painful work. Her death took place in December of the same year (1848) in which Branwell died. Anne, already delicate, would never seem to have held up her head after her sister's death, and in May 1849 she followed, but in all sweetness and calmness, to her early grave. She was twenty-eight; Emily twenty-nine. So soon had the fever of life worn itself out and peace come. Charlotte was left alone. There had not been to her in either of them the close companion which they had found in each other. But yet life ebbed away from her with their deaths, which occurred in such a startling and quick succession as always makes bereavement more terrible.

This occurred at the height of her mental activity. "Shirley" had been published, and had been received with the divided feeling we have referred to; and when she was thus left alone she found, no doubt, the solace which of all mortal things work gives best, by resuming her natural occupation in the now more than ever sombre seclusion of the Parsonage, to which, however, her favourite friend, Ellen Nussey, came from time to time. One or two visits to London occurred after the two first publications in which, a demure little person, silent and shy, yet capable of expressing herself very distinctly by times, and by no means unconscious of the claim she now had upon other people's respect and admiration, Charlotte Brontë made a little sensation in the society which was opened to her, not always of a very successful kind. Everybody will remember the delightfully entertaining chapter in literary history in which Mrs. Ritchie, with charming humour and truth, recounts the visit of this odd little lion to her father's house, and Thackeray's abrupt and clandestine flight to his club when it was found that nothing more was to be made of her than an absorbed conversation with the governess in the back drawing-room, a situation like one in a novel, and so very like the act of modest greatness, singling out the least important person as the object of her attentions.

She is described by all her friends as plain, even ugly—a small woman with a big nose, and no other notable feature, not even the bright eyes which are generally attributed to genius—which was probably, however, better than the lackadaisical portrait prefixed to her biography, after a picture by Richmond, which is the typical portrait of a governess of the old style, a gentle creature deprecating and wistful. Her letters are very good letters, well expressed in something of the old-fashioned way, but without any of the charm of a born letter-writer. Indeed, charm does not seem to have been hers in any way. But she had a few very staunch friends who held fast by her all her life, notwithstanding the uncomfortable experience of being "put in a book," which few people like. It is a gift by itself to put other living people in books. The novelist does not always possess it; to many the realms of imagination are far more easy than the arid realms of fact, and to frame an image of a man much more natural than to take his portrait. I am not sure that it is not a mark of greater strength to be able to put a living and recognisable person on the canvas than it is to invent one. Anyhow, Miss Brontë possessed it in great perfection. Impossible to doubt that the characters of "Shirley" were real men; still more impossible to doubt for a moment the existence of M. Paul Emmanuel. The pursuit of such a system requires other faculties than those of the mere romancist. It demands a very clear-cut opinion, a keen judgment not disturbed by any strong sense of the complexities of nature, nor troubled by any possibility of doing injustice to its victim.

*****

One thing strikes us very strongly in the description of the school, Lowood, which was her very first step in literature, and in which there can now be no doubt, from her own remarks on the manner in which it was received, she had a vindictive purpose. I scarcely know why, for, of course, the dates are all there to prove the difference—but my own conclusion had always been that she was a girl of fourteen or fifteen, old enough to form an opinion when she left the school. I find, with much consternation, that she was only nine; and that so far as such a strenuous opinion was her own at all, it must have been formed at that early and not very judicious age. That the picture should be so vivid with only a little girl's recollection to go upon is wonderful; but it is not particularly valuable as a verdict against a great institution, its founder and all its ways. Nevertheless, it had its scathing and wounding effect as much as if the little observer, whose small judgment worked so precociously, had been capable of understanding the things which she condemned. It would be rash to trust nineteen in such a report, but nine!

It was at a different age and in other circumstances that Charlotte Brontë made her deep and extraordinary study of the Brussels Pensionnat. She was twenty-seven; she had already gone through a number of those years of self-repression during which, by dint of keeping silence, the heart burns. She was, if we may accept the freedom of her utterances in fiction as more descriptive of her mind than the measured sentences of her letters, angry with fate and the world which denied her a brighter career, and bound her to the cold tasks of dependence and the company of despised and almost hated inferiors during the best of her life. Her tremendous gift of sight—not second sight or any visionary way of regarding the object before her, but that vivid and immediate vision which took in every detail, and was decisive on every act as if it had been the vision of the gods—was now fully matured. She saw all that was about her with this extraordinary clearness without any shadow upon the object or possibility of doubt as to her power of seeing it all round and through and through. She makes us also see and know the big white house, with every room distinct: the garden, with its great trees and alleys: the class-rooms, each with its tribune: the girls, fat and round and phlegmatic in characteristic foreignism, and herself as spectator, looking on with contemptuous indifference, not caring to discriminate between them. The few English figures, which concern her more, are drawn keen upon the canvas, though with as little friendliness; the teachers sharply accentuated, Mdlle. Sophie, for instance, who, when she is in a rage, has no lips, and all the sharp contentions and false civilities of those banded Free Lances, enemies to everybody and to each other; the image of watchful suspicion in the head of the house—all these are set forth in glittering lines of steel. There is not a morsel of compunction in the picture. Everybody is bad, worthless, a hater of the whole race. The mistress of the establishment moves about stealthily, watching, her eyes showing through a mist in every corner, going and coming without a sound. What a picture it is! There is not a good meaning in the whole place—not even that beneficent absence of meaning which softens the view. They are all bent on their own aims, on gaining an advantage great or small over their neighbours; nobody is spared, nobody is worth a revision of judgment—except one.

The little Englishwoman herself, who is the centre of all

this, is not represented as more lovable than the rest. She is the hungry little epicure, looking on while others feast, and envying every one of them, even while she snarls at their fare as apples of Gomorrah. She cannot abide that they should be better off than she, even though she scorns their satisfaction in what they possess. Her wild and despairing rush through Brussels when the town is *en fête*, cold, impassioned, fever-hot with rancour and loneliness, produces the most amazing effect on the mind. She is the banished spirit for whom there is no place, the little half-tamed wild beast, wild with desire to tear and rend everything that is happy. One feels that she has a certain justification and realises the full force of being left out in the cold, of having no part or lot in the matter when other people are amused and rejoice. Many other writers have endeavoured to produce a similar effect with milder means, but I suppose because of a feeble-minded desire to preserve the reputation of their forlorn heroine and give the reader an amiable view of her, no one has succeeded like the author of "Villette," who is in no way concerned for the amiability of Lucy Snowe.

For the impartiality of this picture is as extraordinary as its power. Lucy Snowe is her own historian; it is the hot blood of the autobiographist that rushes through her veins, yet no attempt is made to recommend her to the reader or gain his sympathy. She is much too real to think of these outside things, or of how people will judge her, or how to make her proceedings acceptable to their eyes. We do not know whether Charlotte Brontë ever darted out of the white still house, standing dead in the moonlight, and rushed through the streets and, like a ghost, into the very heart of the gaslights and festivities; but it would be difficult to persuade any reader that some one had not done so, imprinting that phantasmagoria of light and darkness upon a living brain. Whether it was Charlotte Brontë or Lucy Snowe, the effect is the same. We are not even asked to feel for her or pity her, much less to approve her. Nothing is demanded from us on her account but merely to behold the soul in revolt and the strange workings of her despair. It was chiefly because of the indifference to her of Dr. John that Lucy was thus driven into a momentary madness; and with the usual regardless indiscretion of all Charlotte Brontë's amateur biographers, Mr. Shorter intimates to us who was the living man who was Dr. John and occasioned all the commotion. The tragedy, however it appears, was unnecessary, for the victim got over it with no great difficulty, and soon began the much more engrossing interest which still remained behind.

Nothing up to this point has attracted us in "Villette," except, indeed, the tremendous vitality and reality of the whole, the sensation of the actual which is in every line, and which forbids us to believe for a moment that what we are reading is fiction. But a very different sentiment comes into being as we become acquainted with the black bullet-head and vivacious irascible countenance of M. Paul Emmanuel. He is the one only character in Miss Brontë's little world who has a real charm, whose entrance upon the stage warms all our feelings and awakens in us not interest alone, but lively liking, amusement and sympathy. The quick-witted, quick-tempered Frenchman, with all the foibles of his vanity displayed, as susceptible to any little slight as a girl, as easily pleased with a sign of kindness, as far from the English ideal as it is possible to imagine, dancing with excitement, raging with displeasure, committing himself by every step he takes, cruel, delightful, barbarous and kind, is set before us in the fullest light, intolerable but always enchanting. He is as full of variety as Rosalind, as devoid of dignity as Pierrot, contradictory, inconsistent, vain, yet conquering all our prejudices and enchanting us while he performs every antic that, according to our usual code, a man ought not to be capable of. How was it that for this once the artist got the better of all her restrictions and overcame all her misconceptions, and gave us a man to be heartily loved, laughed at, and taken into our hearts?

I cannot answer that question. I am sorry that he was M. Héger, and the master of the establishment, and not the clever tutor who had so much of Madame Beck's confidence. But anyhow, he is the best that Miss Brontë ever did for us, the most attractive individual, the most perfect picture. The Rochesters were all more or less fictitious, notwithstanding the unconscious inalienable force of realism which gives them, in spite of themselves and us, a kind of overbearing life; but Miss Brontë never did understand what she did not know. She had to see a thing before it impressed itself upon her, and when she did see it, with what force she saw! She knew M. Paul Emmanuel, watching him day by day, seeing all his littlenesses and childishness, his vanity, his big warm heart, his clever brain, the manifold nature of the man. He stands out, as the curates stood out, absolutely real men about whom we could entertain no doubt, recognisable anywhere. The others were either a woman's men, like the Moors of Shirley, whose roughness was bluster (she could not imagine an Englishman who was not rough and rude), and their strength more or less made up; or an artificial composition like St. John, an ideal bully like Rochester. The ideal was not her forte—she had few gifts that way: but she saw with overwhelming lucidity and keenness, and what she saw, without a doubt, without a scruple, she could put upon the canvas in lines of fire. Seldom, very seldom, did an object appear within reach of that penetrating light, which could be drawn lovingly or made to appear as a being to be loved. Was not the sole model of that species M. Paul? It would seem that in the piteous poverty of her life, which was so rich in natural power, she had never met before a human creature in whom she could completely trust, or one who commended himself to her entirely, with all his foibles and weaknesses increasing, not diminishing, the charm.

It is, in my opinion, a most impertinent inquiry to endeavour to search out what were the sentiments of Charlotte Brontë for M. Héger. Any one whom it would be more impossible to imagine as breaking the very first rule of English decorum, and letting her thoughts stray towards another woman's husband, I cannot imagine. Her fancy was wild and her utterance free, and she liked to think that men were quite untrammelled by those proprieties which bound herself like bonds of iron in her private person, and that she might pluck a fearful joy by listening to their dreadful experiences: but she herself was as prim and Puritan as any little blameless governess that ever went out of an English parish. But while believing this I cannot but feel it was an intolerable spite of fortune that the one manwhom she knew in her life, whom her story could make others love, the only man whom she saw with that real illumination which does justice to humanity, was not M. Paul Emmanuel but M. Héger. This was why we were left trembling at the end of Lucy Snowe's story, not knowing whether he ever came back to her out of the wilds, fearing almost as keenly that nothing but loss could fitly end the tale, yet struggling in our imaginations against the doom—as if it had concerned our own happiness.

Was this new-born power in her, the power of representing a man at his best, she who by nature saw both men and women from their worst side, a sign of the development of genius in herself, the softening of that scorn with which she had hitherto regarded a world chiefly made up of inferior beings, the mellowing influence of maturity? So we might have said, had it not been that after this climax of production she never spake word more in the medium of fiction. Had she told the world everything she had to say? Could she indeed say nothing but what she had seen and known in her limited experience—the trials of school and governessing, the longing of women, the pangs of solitude? That strange form of imagination which can deal only with fact, and depict nothing but what is under its eyes, is in its way perhaps the most impressive of all—especially when inspired by the remorseless lights of that keen outward vision which is unmitigated by any softening of love for the race, any embarrassing toleration as to feelings and motives. It is unfortunately true in human affairs that those who expect a bad ending to everything, and suspect a motive at least dubious to every action, prove right in a great number of cases, and that the qualities of truth and realism have been appropriated to their works by almost universal consent. Indeed there are some critics who think this the only true form of art. But it is at the same time a power with many limitations. The artist who labours, as M. Zola does, searching into every dust-heap, as if he could find out human nature, the only thing worth depicting, with all its closely hidden secrets, all its flying indistinguishable tones, all its infinite gradations of feeling, by that nauseous process, or by a roaring progress through the winds, upon a railway brake, or the visit of a superficial month to the most complicated, the most subtle of cities—must lay up for himself and for his reader many disappointments and deceptions: but the science of artistic study, as exemplified in him, had not been invented in Charlotte Brontë's day.

She did not attempt to go and see things with the intention of representing them; she was therefore limited to the representation of those things which naturally in the course of life came under her eyes. She knew, though only as a child, the management and atmosphere of a great school, and set it forth, branding a great institution with an insufferable stigma, justly or unjustly, who knows? She went to another school and turned out every figure in it for our inspection—a community all jealous, spiteful, suspicious, clandestine: even the chance pupil with no particular relation to her story or herself, painted with all her frivolities for the edification of the world did not escape. "She was Miss So-and-So," say the army of commentators who have followed Miss Brontë, picking up all the threads, so that the grand-daughter of the girl who had the misfortune to be in the Brussels Pensionnat along with that remorseless artist may be able to study the character of her ancestress. The public we fear loves this kind of art, however, notwithstanding all its drawbacks.

On the other hand probably no higher inspiration could have set before us so powerfully the image of M. Paul. Thus we are made acquainted with the best and the worst which can be effected by this method—the base in all their baseness, the excellent all the dearer for their characteristic faults: but the one representation scarcely less offensive than the other to the victim. Would it be less trying to the individual to be thus caught, identified, written out large in the light of love and glowing adoration, than in the more natural light of scorn? I know not indeed which would be the worst ordeal to go through, to be drawn like Madame Beck, suspicious, stealthy, with watchful eyes appearing out of every corner, surprising every incautious word, than to be put upon the scene in the other manner, with all your peccadilloes exposed in the light of admiration and fondness, and yourself put to play the part of hero and lover. The point of view of the public is one thing, that of the victim quite another. We are told that Miss Brontë, perhaps with a momentary compunction for what she had done, believed herself to have prevented all injurious effects by securing that "Villette" should not be published in Brussels, or translated into the French tongue, both of them of course perfectly futile hopes since the very desire to hinder its appearance was a proof that this appearance would be of unusual interest. The fury of the lady exposed in all her stealthy ways could scarcely have been less than the confusion of her spouse when he found himself held up to the admiration of his town as Lucy Snowe's captivating lover. To be sure it may be said the public has nothing to do with this. These individuals are dead and gone, and no exposure can hurt them any longer, whereas the gentle reader lives for ever, and goes on through the generations, handing on to posterity his delight in M. Paul. But all the same it is a cruel and in reality an immoral art; and it has this great disadvantage, that its area is extremely circumscribed, especially when the artist lives most of her life in a Yorkshire parsonage amid the moors, where so few notable persons come in her way.

* * * * *

There was however one subject of less absolute realism which Charlotte Brontë had at her command, having experienced in her own person and seen her nearest friends under the experience, of that solitude and longing of women, of which she has made so remarkable an exposition. The long silence of life without an adventure or a change, the forlorn gaze out at windows which never show any one coming who can rouse the slightest interest in the mind, the endless years and days which pass and pass, carrying away the bloom, extinguishing the lights of youth, bringing a dreary middle age before which the very soul shrinks, while yet the sufferer feels how strong is the current of life in her own veins, and how capable she is of all the active duties of existence—this was the essence and soul of the existence she knew best. Was there no help for it? Must the women wait and long and see their lives thrown away, and have no power to save themselves?

The position in itself so tragic is one which can scarcely be expressed without calling forth an inevitable ridicule, a laugh at the best, more often a sneer at the women whose desire for a husband is thus betrayed. Shirley and Caroline Helston both cried out for that husband with an indignation, a fire and impatience, a sense of wrong and injury, which stopped the laugh for the moment. It might be ludicrous but it was horribly genuine and true. Note there was nothing sensual about these young women. It was life they wanted; they knew nothing of the grosser thoughts which the world with its jeers attributes to them: of such thoughts they were unconscious in a primitive innocence which perhaps only women understand. They wanted their life, their place in the world, the rightful share of women in the scheme of nature. Why did not it come to them? The old patience in which women have lived for all the centuries fails now and again in a keen moment of energy when some one arises who sees no reason why she should endure this forced inaction, or why she should invent for herself inferior ways of working and give up her birthright, which is to carry on the world.

The reader was horrified with these sentiments from the lips of young women. The women were half ashamed, yet more than half stirred and excited by the outcry, which was true enough if indelicate. All very well to talk of women working for their living, finding new channels for themselves, establishing their independence. How much have we said of all that, endeavouring to persuade ourselves! Charlotte Brontë had the courage of her opinions. It was not education nor a trade that her women wanted. It was not a living but their share in life, a much more legitimate object had that been the way to secure it, or had there been any way to secure it in England. Miss Brontë herself said correct things about the protection which a trade is to a woman, keeping her from a mercenary marriage; but this was not in the least the way of her heroines. They wanted to be happy, no doubt, but above all things they wanted their share in life—to have their position by the side of men, which alone confers a natural equality, to have their shoulder to the wheel, their hands on the reins of common life, to build up the world, and link the generations each to each. In her philosophy marriage was the only state which procured this, and if she did not recommend a mercenary marriage she was at least very tolerant about its conditions, insisting less upon love than was to be expected and with a covert conviction in her mind that if not one man then another was better than any complete abandonment of the larger path. Lucy Snowe for a long time had her heart very much set on Dr. John and his placid breadth of Englishism: but when she finally found out that to be impossible her tears were soon dried by the prospect of Paul Emmanuel, so unlike him, coming into his place.

Poor Charlotte Brontë! She has not been as other women, protected by the grave from all betrayal of the episodes in her own life. Everybody has betrayed her, and all she thought about this one and that, and every name that was ever associated with hers. There was a Mr. Taylor from London about whom she wrote with great freedom to her friend Miss Nussey, telling how the little man had come, how he had gone away without any advance in the affairs, how a chill came over her when he appeared and she found him much less attractive than when at a distance, yet how she liked it as little when he went away and was somewhat excited about his first letter, and even went so far as to imagine with a laugh that there might be possibly a dozen little Joe Taylors before all was over. She was hard upon Miss Austen for having no comprehension of passion, but no one could have been cooler and less impassioned than she as she considered the question of Mr. Taylor, reluctant to come to any decision yet disappointed when it came to nothing. There was no longing in her mind for Mr. Taylor, but there was for life and action and the larger paths and the little Joes.

This longing which she expressed with so much vehemence and some poetic fervour as the burden of the lives of Shirley and her friends has been the keynote of a great deal that has followed— the revolts and rebellions, the wild notions about marriage, the "Sex Problem," and a great deal more. From that first point to the prevailing discussion of all the questions involved is a long way; but it is a matter of logical progression, and when once the primary matter is opened, every enlargement of the subject may be taken as a thing to be expected. Charlotte Brontë was in herself the embodiment of all old-fashioned restrictions. She was proper, she was prim, her life was hedged in by all the little rules which bind the primitive woman. But when she left her little recluse behind and rushed into the world of imagination her exposure of the bondage in which she sat with all her sisters was far more daring than if she had been a woman of many experiences and knew what she was speaking of. She did know the longing, the discontent, the universal contradiction and contrariety which is involved in that condition of unfulfilment to which so many grey and undeveloped lives are condemned. For her and her class, which did not speak of it, everything depended upon whether the woman married or did not marry. Their thoughts were thus artificially fixed to one point in the horizon, but their ambition was neither ignoble nor unclean. It was bold, indeed, in proportion to its almost ridiculous innocence, and want of perception of any grosser side. Their share in life, their part in the mutual building of the house, was what they sought. But the seed she thus sowed has come to many growths which would have appalled Charlotte Brontë. Those who took their first inspiration from this cry of hers, have quite forgotten what it was she wanted, which was not emancipation but an extended duty. But while it would be very unjust to blame her for the vagaries that have followed and to which nothing could be less desirable than any building of the house or growth of the race, any responsibility or service—we must still believe that it was she who drew the curtain first aside and opened the gates to imps of evil meaning, polluting and profaning the domestic hearth.

The marriage which—after all these wild embodiments of the longing and solitary heart which could not consent to abandon its share in life, after Shirley and Lucy Snowe, and that complex unity of three female souls all unfulfilled, which had now been broken by death—she accepted in the end of her life, is the strangest commentary upon all that went before, or rather, upon all the literary and spiritual part of her history, though it was a quite appropriate ending to Mr. Brontë's daughter, and even to the writer of those sober letters which discussed Mr. Taylor, whether he should or should not be encouraged, and how it was a little disappointing after all to see him go away. Her final suitor was one of the class which she had criticised so scathingly, one who, it might have been thought, would scarcely have ventured to enter the presence or brave the glance of so penetrating an eye, but who would seem to have brought all the urgency of a *grand passion* to the sombre parlour of the parsonage, to the afternoon stillness of the lonely woman who would not seem to have suspected anything of the kind till it was poured out before her without warning. She was startled and confused by his declaration and appeal, never apparently having contemplated the possibility of any such occurrence; and in the interval which followed the father raged and resisted, and the lover did not conceal his heartbroken condition but suffered without complaining while the lady looked on wistful, touched and attracted by the unlooked-for love, and gradually melting towards that, though indifferent to the man who offered it. Mr. Brontë evidently thought that if this now distinguished daughter who had been worshipped among the great people in London, and talked of in all the newspapers, married at all in her mature age, it should be some one distinguished like herself, and not the mere curate who was the natural fate of every clergyman's daughter, the simplest and least known.

Charlotte meanwhile said no word, but saw the curate enact various tragic follies of love for her sake with a sort of awe and wonder, astonished to find herself thus possessed still of the charm which none are so sure as women that only youth and beauty can be expected to possess. And she had never had any beauty, and, though she was not old, was no longer young. It is a conventional fiction that a woman still in the thirties is beyond the exercise of that power. Indeed, it would be hard to fix the age at which the spell departs. Certainly the demeanour of Mr. Nicholls gave her full reason to believe that it had not departed from her. He faltered in the midst of the service, grew pale, almost lost his self-possession when he suddenly saw her among the kneeling figures round the altar; and no doubt this rather shocking and startling exhibition of his feelings was more pardonable to the object of so much emotion than it was likely to have been to any other spectator. The romance is a little strange, but yet it is a romance in its quaint ecclesiastical way. And soon Charlotte was drawn still more upon her lover's side by the violence of her father. It was decided that the curate was to go, and that this late gleam of love-making was to be extinguished and the old dim atmosphere to settle down again for ever. Finally, however, the mere love of love, which had always been more to her than any personal inclination, and the horror of that permanent return to the twilight of dreamy living against which she had struggled all her life, overcame her, and gave her courage; but she married characteristically, not as women marry who are carried to a new home and make a new beginning in life, but retaining all the circumstances of the old and receiving her husband into her father's house where she had already passed through so many fluctuations and dreamed so many dreams, and which was full to overflowing with the associations of the past.

We have no reason to suppose that it did not add to the happiness of her life; indeed, every indication is to the contrary, and the husband seems to have been kind, considerate and affectionate. Still this thing upon which so many of her thoughts had been fixed during her whole life, which she had felt to be the necessary condition of full development, and for which the little impassioned female circle of which she was the expositor had sighed and cried to heaven and earth, came to her at last very much in the form of a catastrophe. No doubt the circumstances of her quickly failing health and shortened life promote this feeling. But without really taking these into consideration the sensation remains the same. The strange little keen soul with its sharply fixed restrictions, yet intense force of perception within its limits, dropped out of the world into which it had made an irruption so brilliant and so brief and sank out of sight altogether, sank into the humdrum house between the old father and the sober husband, into the clerical atmosphere with which she had no sympathy, into the absolute quiet of domestic life to which no Prince Charming could now come gaily round the corner, out of the mists and moors, and change with a touch of his wand the grey mornings and evenings into golden days. Well! was not this that which she had longed for, the natural end of life towards which her Shirley, her Caroline, her Lucy had angrily stretched forth their hands, indignant to be kept waiting, clamouring for instant entrance? And so it was, but how different! Lucy Snowe's little housekeeping, all the preparations which M. Paul made for her comfort and which seemed better to her than any palace, would not they too have taken the colour of perpetual dulness if everything had settled down and the Professor assumed his slippers by the domestic hearth? Ah no, for Lucy Snowe loved the man, and Charlotte Brontë, as appears, loved only the love. It is a parable. She said a little later that she began to see that this was the fate which she would wish for those she loved best, for her friend Ellen, perhaps for her Emily if she had lived—the good man very faithful, very steady, worth his weight in gold—yet flatter than the flattest days of old, *solidement nourri*, a good substantial husband, managing all the parish business, full of talk about the Archdeacon's charge, and the diocesan meetings, and the other clergy of the moorland parishes. We can conceive that she got to fetching his slippers for him and taking great care that he was comfortable, and perhaps had it been so ordained might have grown into a contented matron and forgotten the glories and miseries, so inseparably twined and linked together, of her youth. But she only had a year in which to do all that, and this is how her marriage seems to turn into a catastrophe, the caging of a wild creature that had never borne captivity before, and which now could no longer rush forth into the heart of any shining *fête*, or to the window of a strange confessional, anywhere, to throw off the burden of the perennial contradiction, the ceaseless unrest of the soul, the boilings of the volcano under the snow.

* * * * *

I have said it was difficult to account for the extreme interest still attaching to everything connected with Charlotte Brontë; not only the story of her peculiar genius, but also of everybody connected with her, though the circle was in reality quite a respectable, humdrum, and uninteresting one, containing nobody of any importance except the sister, who was her own wilder and fiercer part. One way, however, in which these sisters have won some part of their long-lasting interest is due to the treatment to which they have been subjected. They are the first victims of that ruthless art of biography which is one of the features of our time; and that not only by Mrs. Gaskell, who took up her work in something of an apologetic vein, and was so anxious to explain how it was that her heroine expressed certain ideas not usual in the mouths of women, that she was compelled to take away the reputation of a number of other people in order to excuse the peculiarities of these two remarkable women. But everybody who has touched their history since, and there have been many—for it would seem that gossip, when restrained by no bonds of decorum or human feeling, possesses a certain interest whether it is concerned with the household of a cardinal or that of a parish priest—has followed the same vicious way without any remonstrance or appeal for mercy. We have all taken it for granted that no mercy was to be shown to the Brontës. Let every rag be torn from Charlotte, of whom there is the most to say. Emily had the good luck to be no correspondent, and so has escaped to some degree the complete exposure of every confidence and every thought which has happened to her sister. Is it because she has nobody to defend her that she has been treated thus barbarously? I cannot conceive a situation more painful, more lacerating to every feeling, than that of the father and the husband dwelling silent together in that sombre parsonage, from which every ray of light seems to depart with the lost woman, whose presence had kept a little savour in life, and looking on in silence to see their life taken to pieces, and every decent veil dragged from the inner being of their dearest and nearest. They complained as much as two voiceless persons could, or at least the father complained: and the very servants came hot from their kitchen to demand a vindication of their character: but nobody noted the protest of the old man amid the silence of the moors: and the husband was more patient and spoke no word. Even he, however, after nearly half a century, when that far-off episode of life must have become dim to him, has thrown his relics open for a little more revelation, a little more interference with the helpless ashes of the dead.

No dot is now omitted upon i, no t left uncrossed. We know, or at least are told, who Charlotte meant by every character she ever portrayed, even while the model still lives. We know her opinion of her friends, or rather acquaintances, the people whom she saw cursorily and formed a hasty judgment upon, as we all do in the supposed safety of common life. Protests have been offered in other places against a similar treatment of other persons; but scarcely any protest has been attempted in respect to Charlotte Brontë. The resurrection people have been permitted to make their researches as they pleased. It throws a curious pathos, a not unsuitably tragic light upon a life always so solitary, that this should all have passed in silence because there was actually no one to interfere, no one to put a ban upon the dusty heaps and demand that no mere should be said. When one looks into the matter a little more closely, one finds it is so with almost all those who have specially suffered at the hands of the biographer. The Carlyles had no child, no brother to rise up in their defence. It gives the last touch of melancholy to the conclusion of a lonely life. Mrs. Gaskell, wise woman, defended herself from a similar treatment by will, and left children behind her to protect her memory. But the Brontës are at the mercy of every one who cares to give another raking to the diminished heap of *débris*. The last writer who has done so, Mr. Clement Shorter, had some real new light to throw upon a story which surely has now been sufficiently turned inside out, and has done his work withperfect good feeling, and, curiously enough after so many exploitations, in a way which shows that interest has not yet departed from the subject. But we trust that now the memory of Charlotte Brontë will be allowed to rest.

An Excerpt From
Women Novelists of Queen Victoria's Reign
- A Book of Appreciations, 1897

HAWORTH

BY VIRGINIA WOOLF

Haworth was the home of the Brontë family. Virginia Woolf's account of a visit to Haworth was the first of her writings to be accepted for publication (and the second to appear in print.) Woolf's article was first published in The Guardian, unsigned, on 21st December, 1904.

I do not know whether pilgrimages to the shrines of famous men ought not to be condemned as sentimental journeys. It is better to read Carlyle in your own study chair than to visit the sound-proof room and pore over the manuscripts at Chelsea. I should be inclined to set up an examination on Frederick the Great in place of an entrance fee; only, in that case, the house would soon have to be shut up. The curiosity is only legitimate when the house of a great writer or the country in which it is set adds something to our understanding of his books. This justification you have for a pilgrimage to the home and country of Charlotte Brontë and her sisters.

The *Life*, by Mrs Gaskell, gives you the impression that Haworth and the Brontës are somehow inextricably mixed. Haworth expresses the Brontës; the Brontës express Haworth; they fit like a snail to its shell. How far surroundings radically affect people's minds, it is not for me to ask: superficially, the influence is great, but it is worth asking if the famous parsonage had been placed in a London slum, the dens of Whitechapel would not have had the same result as the lonely Yorkshire moors. However, I am taking away my only excuse for visiting Haworth. Unreasonable or not, one of the chief points of a recent visit to Yorkshire was that an expedition to Haworth could be accomplished. The necessary arrangements were made, and we determined to take advantage of the first day for our expedition. A real northern snowstorm had been doing the honours of the moors. It was rash to wait fine weather, and it was also cowardly. I understand that the sun very seldom shone on the Brontë family, and if we chose a really fine day we should have to make allowance for the fact that fifty years ago there were few fine days at Haworth, and that we were, therefore, for sake of comfort, rubbing out half the shadows on the picture. However, it would be interesting to see what impression Haworth could make upon the brilliant weather of Settle. We certainly passed through a very cheerful land, which might be likened to a vast wedding cake, of which the icing was slightly undulating; the earth was bridal in its virgin snow, which helped to suggest the comparison.

Keighley - pronounced Keethly - is often mentioned in the *Life*; it was the big town four miles from Haworth in which Charlotte walked to make her more important purchases - her wedding gown, perhaps, and the thin little cloth boots which we examined under glass in the Brontë Museum. It is a big manufacturing town, hard and stony, and clattering with business, in the way of these Northern towns. They make small provision for the sentimental traveller, and our only occupation was to picture the slight figure of Charlotte trotting along the streets in her thin mantle, hustled into the gutter by more burly passers-by. It was the Keighley of her day, and that was some comfort. Our excitement as we neared Haworth had in it an element of suspense that was really painful, as though we were to meet some long-separated friend, who might have changed in the interval - so clear an image of Haworth had we from print and picture. At a certain point we entered the valley, up both sides of which the village climbs, and right on the hill-top, looking down over its parish, we saw the famous oblong tower of the church. This marked the shrine at which we were to do homage.

It may have been the effect of a sympathetic imagination, but I think that there were good reasons why Haworth did certainly strike one not exactly as gloomy, but, what is worse for artistic purposes, as dingy and commonplace. The houses, built of yellow-brown stone, date from the early nineteenth century. They climb the moor step by step in little detached strips, some distance apart, so that the town instead of making one compact blot on the landscape has contrived to get a whole stretch into its clutches. There is a long line of houses up the moor-side, which clusters round the church and parsonage with a little clump of trees. At the top the interest for a Brontë lover becomes suddenly intense. The church, the parsonage, the Brontë Museum, the school where Charlotte taught, and the Bull Inn where Branwell drank are all within a stone's throw of each other. The museum is certainly rather a pallid and inanimate collection of objects. An effort ought to be made to keep things out of these mausoleums, but the choice often lies between them and destruction, so that we must be grateful for the care which has preserved much that is, under any circumstances, of deep interest. Here are many autograph letters, pencil drawings, and other documents. But the most touching case - so touching that one hardly feels reverent in one's gaze - is that which contains the little personal relics of the dead woman. The natural fate of such things is to die before the body that wore them, and because these, trifling and transient though they are, have survived, Charlotte Brontë the woman comes to life, and one forgets the chiefly memorable fact that she was a great writer. Her shoes and her thin muslin dress have outlived her. One other object gives a thrill; the little oak stool which Emily carried with her on her solitary moorland tramps, and on which she sat, if not to write, as they say, to think what was probably better than her writing.

The church, of course, save part of the tower, is renewed since Brontë days; but that remarkable churchyard remains. The old edition of the *Life* had on its title-page a little print which struck the keynote of the book; it seemed to be all graves - gravestones stood ranked all round; you walked on a pavement lettered with dead names; the graves had solemnly invaded the garden of the parsonage itself, which was as a little oasis of life in the midst of the dead. This is no exaggeration of the artist's, as we found: the stones seem to start out of the ground at you in tall, upright lines, like and army of silent soldiers. there is no hand's breadth untenanted; indeed, the economy of space is somewhat irreverent. In old days a flagged path, which suggested the slabs of graves, led from the front door of the parsonage to the churchyard without interruption of wall or hedge; the garden was practically the graveyard too; the successors of the Brontës, however, wishing a little space between life and death, planted a hedge and several tall trees, which now cut off the parsonage garden completely. The house itself is precisely the same as it was in Charlotte's day, save that one new wing has been added. It is easy to shut the eye to this, and then you have the square, boxlike parsonage, built of the ugly yellow-brown stone which they quarry from the moors behind, precisely as it was when Charlotte lived and died there. Inside, of course, the changes are many, though not such as to obscure the original shape of the rooms. There is nothing remarkable in a mid-Victorian parsonage, though tenanted by genius, and the only room which awakens curiosity is the kitchen, now used as an ante-room, in which the girls tramped as they conceived their work. One other spot has a certain grim interest - the oblong recess beside the staircase into which Emily drove her bulldog during the famous fight, and pinned him while she pommelled him. It is otherwise a little sparse parsonage, much like others of its kind. It was due to the courtesy of the present incumbent that we were allowed to inspect it; in his place I should often feel inclined to exorcise the three famous ghosts.

One thing only remained: the church in which Charlotte worshipped, was married, and lies buried. The circumference of her life was very narrow. Here, though much is altered, a few things remain to tell of her. The slab which bears the names of the succession of children and of their parents - their births and deaths - strikes the eye first. Name follows name; at very short intervals they died - Maria the mother, Maria the daughter, Elizabeth, Branwell, Emily, Anne, Charlotte, and lastly the old father, who outlived them all. Emily was only thirty years old, and Charlotte but nine years older. 'The sting of death is sin, and the strength of sin is the law, but thanks be to God which giveth us the victory through our Lord Jesus Christ.' That is the inscription which has been placed beneath their names, and with reason; for however harsh the struggle, Emily, and Charlotte above all, fought to victory.

AN EXCERPT FROM
The Guardian, 1904

EMILY BRONTË

BY ARTHUR SYMONS

This was a woman young and passionate,
Loving the Earth, and loving most to be
Where she might be alone with liberty;
Loving the beasts, who are compassionate;
The homeless moors, her home; the bright elate
Winds of the cold dawn; rock and stone and tree;
Night, bringing dreams out of eternity;
And memory of Death's unforgetting date.
She too was unforgetting: has she yet
Forgotten that long agony when her breath
Too fierce for living fanned the flame of death?
Earth for her heather, does she now forget
What pity knew not in her love from scorn,
And that it was an unjust thing to be born?

The Stoic in woman has been seen once only, and that in the only woman in whom there has been seen the paradox of passion without sensuousness. Emily Brontë lived with an unparalleled energy a life of outward quiet, in a loneliness which she shared only with the moors and with the animals whom she loved. She required no passion-experience to endow her with more than a memory of passion. Passion was alive in her as flame is alive in the earth. And the vehemence of that inner fire fed on itself, and wore out her body before its time, because it had no respite and no outlet. We see her condemned to self-imprisonment, and dying of too much life.

Her poems are few and brief, and nothing more personal has ever been written. A few are as masterly in execution as in conception, and almost all have a direct truth of utterance, which rarely lacks at least the bare beauty of muscle and sinew, of a kind of naked strength and alertness. They are without heat or daylight, the sun is rarely in them, and then 'blood-red'; light comes as starshine, or comes as

> Hostile light
> That does not warm but burn.

At times the landscape in this bare, grey, craggy verse, always a landscape of Yorkshire moors, with its touches of stern and tender memory, 'The mute bird sitting on the stone,' 'A little and a lone green lane,' has a quality more thrilling than that of Wordsworth. There is none of his observation, and none of his sense of a benignant 'presence far more deeply interfused'; but there is the voice of the heart's roots, crying out to its home in the earth.

At first this unornamented verse may seem forbidding, may seem even to be ordinary, as an actual moorland may, to those for whom it has no special attraction. But in the verse, as on the moors, there is space, wind, and the smell of the earth; and there is room to be alone, that liberty which this woman cried for when she cried:

> Leave the heart that now I bear,
> And give me liberty.

To be alone was for her to be alone with 'a chainless soul,' which asked of whatever powers might be only 'courage to endure,' constancy not to forget, and the right to leave the door wide open to those visions that came to her out of mere fixed contemplation: 'the God of Visions,' as she called her imagination, 'my slave, my comrade, and my king.' And we know that her courage was flawless, heroic, beyond praise; that she forgot nothing, not even that love for her unspeakable brother, for whom she has expressed in two of her poems a more than masculine magnanimity of pity and contempt; and that at all times she could turn inward to that world within, where her imagination waited for her,

> Where thou, and I, and Liberty
> Have undisputed sovereignty.

Yet even imagination, though 'benignant,' is to her a form of 'phantom bliss' to which she will not trust herself wholly. 'So hopeless is the world without': but is the world within ever quite frankly accepted as a substitute, as a truer reality? She is always on her guard against imagination as against the outer world, whose 'lies' she is resolved shall not 'beguile' her. She has accepted reason as the final arbiter, and desires only to see clearly, to see things as they are. She really believed that

> Earth reserves no blessing
> For the unblest of heaven;

and she had an almost Calvinistic sense of her own condemnation to unhappiness. That being so, she was suspicious of those opportunities of joy which did come to her, or at least resolute not to believe too implicitly in the good messages of the stars, which might be mere dreams, or of the earth, which was only certainly kind in preparing for her that often-thought-of grave. 'No coward soul is mine' is one of her true sayings; but it was with difficulty that she trusted even that message of life which she seemed to discover in death. She has to assure herself of it, again and again: 'Who once lives, never dies!' And that sense of personal identity which aches throughout all her poems is a sense, not of the delight, but of the pain and ineradicable sting of personal identity.

Her poems are all outcries, as her great novel, *Wuthering*

Heights, is one long outcry. A soul on the rack seems to make itself heard at moments, when suffering has grown too acute for silence. Every poem is as if torn from her. Even when she does not write seemingly in her own person, the subjects are such disguises as 'The Prisoner,' 'Honour's Martyr,' 'The Outcast Mother,' echoes of all the miseries and useless rebellions of the earth. She spells over the fading characters in dying faces, unflinchingly, with an austere curiosity; and looks[Pg 114] closely into the eyes of shame, not dreading what she may find there. She is always arguing with herself, and the answers are inflexible, the answers of a clear intellect which rebels but accepts defeat. Her doubt is itself an affirmation, her defiance would be an entreaty but for the 'quenchless will' of her pride. She faces every terror, and to her pained apprehension birth and death and life are alike terrible. Only Webster's dirge might have been said over her coffin.

> What my soul bore my soul alone
> Within itself may tell,

she says truthfully; but some of that long endurance of her life, in which exile, the body's weakness, and a sense of some 'divinest anguish' which clung about the world and all things living, had their share, she was able to put into ascetic and passionate verse. It is sad-coloured and desolate, but when gleams of sunlight or of starlight pierce the clouds that hang generally above it, a rare and stormy beauty comes into the bare outlines, quickening them with living splendour.

An Excerpt From
Figures of Several Centuries, 1906

A WOMAN YOUNG AND PASSIONATE

EMILY BRONTË

BY JOHN COWPER POWYS

The name of Emily Brontë—why does it produce in one's mind so strange and startling a feeling, unlike that produced by any other famous writer?

It is not easy to answer such a question. Certain great souls seem to gather to themselves, as their work accumulates its destined momentum in its voyage down the years, a power of arousing our imagination to issues that seem larger than those which can naturally be explained as proceeding inevitably from their tangible work.

Our imagination is roused and our deepest soul stirred by the mention of such names without any palpable accompaniment of logical analysis, without any well-weighed or rational justification.

Such names touch some response in us which goes deeper than our critical faculties, however desperately they may struggle. Instinct takes the place of reason; and our soul, as if answering the appeal of some translunar chord of subliminal music, vibrates in response to a mood that baffles all analysis.

We all know the work of Emily's sister Charlotte; we know it and can return to it at will, fathoming easily and at leisure the fine qualities of it and its impassioned and romantic effect upon us.

But though we may have read over and over again that one amazing story—"Wuthering Heights"—and that handful of unforgettable poems which are all that Emily Brontë has bequeathed to the world, which of us can say that the full significance of these things has been ransacked and combed out by our conscious reason; which of us can say that we understand to the full all the mysterious stir and ferment, all the far-reaching and magical reactions, which such things have produced within us?

Who can put into words the secret of this extraordinary girl? Who can define, in the suave and plausible language of academic culture, the flitting shadows thrown from deep to deep in the unfathomable genius of her vision?

Perhaps not since Sappho has there been such a person. Certainly she makes the ghosts of de Staël and Georges Sand, of Eliot and Mrs. Browning, look singularly homely and sentimental.

I am inclined to think that the huge mystery of Emily Brontë's power lies in the fact that she expresses in her work—just as the Lesbian, did—the very soul of womanhood. It is not an easy thing to achieve, this. Women writers, clever and lively and subtle, abound in our time, as they have abounded in times past; but for some inscrutable reason they lack the demonic energy, the occult spiritual force, the instinctive fire, wherewith to give expression to the ultimate mystery of their own sex.

I am inclined to think that, of all poets, Walt Whitman is the only one who has drawn his reckless and chaotic inspiration straight from the uttermost spiritual depths of the sex-instincts of the male animal; and Emily Brontë has done for her sex what Walt Whitman did for his.

It is a strange and startling commentary upon the real significance of our sexual impulses that, when it comes to the final issue, it is not the beautiful ruffianism of a Byron, full of normal sex-instinct though that may be, or the eloquent sentiment of a Georges Sand, penetrated with passionate sensuality as that is, which really touch the indefinable secret. Emily Brontë, like Walt Whitman, sweeps us, by sheer force of inspired genius, into a realm where the mere *animalism* of sexuality, its voluptuousness, its lust, its lechery, are absolutely merged, lost, forgotten; fused by that burning flame of spiritual passion into something which is beyond all earthly desire.

Emily Brontë—and this is indicative of the difference between woman and man—goes even further than Walt Whitman in the spiritualising of this flame. In Whitman there is, as we all know, a vast mass of work, wherein, true and magical though it is, the earthly and bodily elements of the great passion are given enormous emphasis. It is only at rare moments—as happens with ordinary men in the normal experience of the world—that he is swept away beyond the reach of lust and voluptuousness. But Emily Brontë seems to dwell by natural predilection upon these high summits and in these unsounded depths. The flame of the passion in her burns at such quivering vibrant pressure that the fuel of it—the debris and rubble of our earth-instincts—is entirely absorbed and devoured. In her work the fire of life licks up, with its consuming tongue, every vestige of materiality in the thing upon which it feeds, and the lofty tremulous spires of its radiant burning ascend into the illimitable void.

It is of extraordinary interest, as a mere psychological phenomenon, to note the fact that when the passion of sex is driven forward by the flame of its conquering impulse beyond a certain point it becomes itself transmuted and loses the earthy texture of its original character.

Sex-passion when carried to a certain pitch of intensity loses its sexuality. It becomes pure flame; immaterial, unearthly, and with no sensual dross left in it.

It may even be said, by an enormous paradox, to become sexless. And this is precisely what one feels about the work of Emily Brontë. Sex-passion in her has been driven so far that it has come round "full circle" and has become sexless passion. It has become passion disembodied, passion absolute, passion divested of all human weakness.

The "muddy vesture of decay" which "grossly closes in" our diviner principle has been burnt up and absorbed. It has been reduced to nothing; and in its place quivers up to heaven the clear white flame of the secret fountain of life.

But there is more in the matter than that. Emily Brontë's genius, by its abandonment to the passion of which I have been speaking, does not only burn up and destroy all the elements of clay in what, so to speak, is above the earth and on its surface; but it also, burning downwards, destroys and annihilates all dubious and obscure materials which surround the original and primordial human will. Round and about this lonely and inalienable will it makes a scorched and blackened plain of ashes and cinders. Ambiguous feelings are turned to ashes there; and so are doubts, hesitations, timidities, trepidations, cowardices. The aboriginal will of man, of the unconquerable individual, stands alone there in the twilight, under the grey desolate rain of the outer spaces. Four-square it stands, upon adamantine foundations, and nothing in heaven or earth is able to shake it or disquiet it.

It is this isolation, in desolate and forlorn integrity, of the individual human will, which is the deepest element in Emily Brontë's genius. Upon this all depends, and to this all returns. Between the will and the spirit deep and strange nuptials are celebrated; and from the immortality of the spirit a certain breath of life passes over into the mortality of the will, drawing it up into the celestial and invisible region which is beyond chance and change.

From this abysmal fusion of the "creator spiritus" with the human will rises that adamantine courage with which Emily Brontë was able to face the jagged edges of that crushing wheel of destiny which the malign powers of nature drive remorselessly over our poor flesh and blood. The uttermost spirit of the universe became in this manner *her* spirit, and the integral identity of the soul within her breast hardened into an undying resistance to all that would undermine it.

Thus she was able to endure tragedy upon tragedy without flinching. Thus she was able to assert herself against the power of pain as one wrestling invincibly with an exhausted giant.

Calamity after calamity fell upon her house, and the stark desolation of those melancholy Yorkshire hills became a suitable and congruous background for the loneliness of her strange life; but against all the pain which came upon her, against all the aching pangs of remorseless fate, this indomitable girl held grimly to her supreme vision.

No poet, no novelist who has ever lived has been so profoundly affected by the conditions of his life as was this invincible woman. But the conditions of her life—the scenery of sombre terror which surrounded her—only touched and affected the outward colour and rhythm of her unique style. In her deepest soul, in the courage of her tremendous vision, she possessed something that was not bounded by Yorkshire hills, or any other hills; something that was inhuman, eternal and universal, something that was outside the power of both time and space.

By that singular and forlorn scenery—the scenery of the Yorkshire moors round about her home—she was, however, in the more flexible portion of her curious nature inveterately influenced. She does not precisely describe this scenery—not at any rate at any length—either in her poems or in "Wuthering Heights"; but it sank so deeply into her that whatever she wrote was affected by it and bears its desolate and imaginative imprint.

It is impossible to read Emily Brontë anywhere without being transported to those Yorkshire moors. One smells the smell of burning furze, one tastes the resinous breath of pine-trees, one feels beneath one's feet the tough fibrous stalks of the ling and the resistant stems and crumpled leaves of the bracken.

Dark against that pallid greenish light of a dead sunset, which is more than anything else characteristic of those unharvested fells, one can perceive always, as one reads her, the sombre form of some gigantic Scotch-fir stretching out its arms across the sky; while a flight of rooks, like enormous black leaves drifting on the wind, sail away into the sunset at our approach.

One is conscious, as one reads her, of lonely marsh-pools turning empty faces towards a grey heaven, while drop by drop upon their murky waters the autumn rain falls, sadly, wearily, without aim or purpose.

And most of all is one made aware of the terrible desolation—desolation only rendered more desolate by the presence of humanity—of those half-ruined farm-houses, approached by windy paths or deep-cut lanes, which seem to rise, like huge fungoid things, here and there over that sad land.

It is difficult to conceive they have not sprung—these dwellings of these Earnshaws and Lintons—actually out of the very soil, in slow organic growth leading to slow organic decay. One cannot conceive the human hands which *built* them; any more than one can conceive the human hands which planted those sombre hedges which have now become so completely part of the scenery that one thinks of them as quite as aboriginal to the place as the pine-trees or the gorse-bushes.

Of all shapes of all trees I think the shape of an old and twisted thorn-tree harmonises best with one's impression of the "milieu" of Emily Brontë's single tragic story; a thorn-tree distorted by the wind blowing from one particular quarter, and with its trunk blackened and hollowed; and in the hollow of it a little pool of rain-water and a few dead soaked leaves.

The extraordinary thing is that she can produce these impressions incidentally, and, as it were, unconsciously. They are so blent with her spirit, these things, that they convey themselves to one's mind indirectly and through a medium far more subtle than any eloquent description.

I cannot think of Emily Brontë's work without thinking of a certain tree I once saw against a pallid sky. A long way from Yorkshire it was where I saw this tree, and there were no limestone boulders scattered at its feet; but something in the impression it produced upon me—an impression I shall not lightly forget—weaves itself strangely in with all I feel about her, so that the peculiar look of wintry boughs, sad and silent against a fading west, accompanied by that natural human longing of people who are tired to be safely buried under the friendly earth and "free among the dead," has come to be most indelibly and deeply associated with her tragic figure.

Those who know those Yorkshire moors know the mysterious way in which the quiet country lanes suddenly emerge upon wide and desolate expanses; know how they lead us on, past ruined factories and deserted quarries, up the barren slopes of forlorn hills; know how, as one sees in front of one the long white road vanishing over the hill-top and losing itself in the grey sky, there comes across one's mind a strange, sad, exquisite feeling unlike any other feeling in the world; and we who love Emily Brontë know that this is the feeling, the mood, the atmosphere of the soul, into which her writings throw us.

The power of her great single story, "Wuthering Heights," is in a primary sense the power of romance, and none can care for this book for whom romance means nothing.

What is romance? I think it is the instinctive recognition of a certain poetic glamour which an especial kind of grouping of persons and things—of persons and things seen under a particular light—is able to produce. It does not always accompany the expression of passionate emotion or the narration of thrilling incidents. These may arrest and entertain us when there is no romance, in my sense at any rate of that great word, overshadowing the picture.

I think this quality of romance can only be evoked when the background of the story is heavily laden with old, rich, dim, pathetic, human associations. I think it can only emerge when there is an implication of thickly mingled traditions, full of sombre and terrible and beautiful suggestiveness, stimulating to the imagination like a draught of heavy red wine. I think there must be, in a story of which the flavour has the true romantic magic, something darkly and inexplicably fatal. I think it is necessary that one should hear the rush of the flight of the Valkyries and the wailing upon the wind of the voices of the Eumenides.

Fate—in such a story—must assume a half-human, half-personal shape, and must brood, obscurely and sombrely, over the incidents and the characters.

The characters themselves must be swayed and dominated by Fate; and not only by Fate. They must be penetrated through and through by the scenery which surrounds them and by the traditions, old and dark and superstitious and malign, of some particular spot upon the earth's surface.

The scenery which is the background of a tale which has the true romantic quality must gather itself together and concentrate itself in some kind of symbolic unity; and this symbolic unity—wherein the various elements of grandeur and mystery are merged—must present itself as something almost personal and as a dynamic "motif" in the development of the plot.

There can be no romance without some sort of appeal to that long-inherited and atavistic feeling in ordinary human hearts which is responsive to the spell and influence of old, unhappy, lovely, ancient things; things faded and falling, but with the mellowness of the centuries upon their faces.

In other words, nothing can be romantic which is *new*. Romance implies, above everything else, a long association with the human feelings of many generations. It implies an appeal to that background of our minds which is stirred to reciprocity by suggestions dealing with those old, dark, mysterious memories which belong, not so much to us as individuals, as to us as links in a great chain.

There are certain emotions in all of us which go much further and deeper than our mere personal feelings. Such are the emotions roused in us by contact with the mysterious forces of life and death and birth and the movements of the seasons; with the rising and setting of the sun, and the primordial labour of tilling the earth and gathering in the harvest. These things have been so long associated with our human hopes and fears, with the nerves and fibres of our inmost being, that any powerful presentment of them brings to the surface the accumulated feelings of hundreds of centuries.

New problems, new adventures, new social groupings, new philosophical catchwords, may all have their vivid and exciting interest. They cannot carry with them that sad, sweet breath of planetary romance which touches what might be called the "imagination of the race" in individual men and women.

"Wuthering Heights" is a great book, not only because of the intensity of the passions in it, but because these passions are penetrated so profoundly with the long, bitter, tragic, human associations of persons who have lived for generations upon the same spot and have behind them the weight of the burden of the sorrows of the dead.

It is a great book because the romance of it emerges into undisturbed amplitude of space, and asserts itself in large, grand, primitive forms unfretted by teasing irrelevancies.

The genius of a romantic novelist—indeed, the genius of all writers primarily concerned with the mystery of human character—consists in letting the basic differences between man and man, between man and woman, rise up, unimpeded by frivolous detail, from the fathomless depths of life itself.

The solitude in which Emily Brontë lived, and the austere simplicity of her granite-moulded character, made it possible for her to envisage life in larger, simpler, less blurred outlines than most of us are able to do. Thus her art has something of that mysterious and awe-inspiring simplicity that characterises the work of Michelangelo or William Blake.

No one who has ever read "Wuthering Heights" can forget the place and the time when he read it. As I write its name now, every reader of this page will recall, with a sudden heavy sigh at the passing of youth, the moment when the sweet tragic power of its deadly genius first took him by the throat.

For me the shadow of an old bowed acacia-tree, held together by iron bands, was over the history of Heathcliff; but the forms and shapes of that mad drama gathered to themselves the lineaments of all my wildest dreams.

I can well remember, too, how on a certain long straight

road between Heathfield and Burwash, the eastern district of Sussex, my companion—the last of our English theologians—turned suddenly from his exposition of St. Thomas, and began quoting, as the white dust rose round us at the passing of a flock of sheep, the "vain are the thousand creeds—unutterably vain!" of that grand and absolute defiance, that last challenge of the unconquerable soul, which ends with the sublime cry to the eternal spark of godhead in us all—

"Thou, thou art being and breath;
And what thou art can never be destroyed!"

The art of Emily Brontë—if it can be called art, this spontaneous projection, in a shape rugged and savage, torn with the storms of fate, of her inmost identity—can be appreciated best if we realise with what skill we are plunged into the dark stream of the destiny of these people through the mediatory intervention of a comparative stranger. By this method, and also by the crafty manner in which she makes the old devoted servant of the house of Earnshaw utter a sort of Sophoclean commentary upon the events which take place, we are permitted to feel the magnitude of the thing in true relief and perspective.

By these devices we have borne in upon us, as in no other way could be done, the convincing sense which we require, to give weight and mass to the story, of the real continuity of life in those savage places.

By this method of narration we have the illusion of being suddenly initiated into a stream of events which are not merely imaginary. We have the illusion that these Earnshaws and Lintons are really, actually, palpably, undeniably, living—living somewhere, in their terrible isolation, as they have always lived—and that it is only by some lucky chance of casual discovery that we have been plunged into the mystery of their days.

One cannot help feeling aware, as we follow the story of Heathcliff, how Emily Brontë has torn and rent at her own soul in the creation of this appalling figure. Heathcliff, without father or mother, without even a Christian name, becomes for us a sort of personal embodiment of the suppressed fury of Emily Brontë's own soul. The cautious prudence and hypocritical reserves of the discreet world of timid, kindly, compromising human beings has got upon the nerves of this formidable girl, and, as she goes tearing and rending at all the masks which cover our loves and our hates, she seems to utter wild discordant cries, cries like those of some she-wolf rushing through the herd of normal human sheep.

Heathcliff and Cathy, what a pair they are! What terrifying lovers! They seem to have arisen from some remote unfathomed past of the world's earlier and less civilised passions. And yet, one occasionally catches, as one goes through the world, the Heathcliff look upon the face of a man and the Cathy look upon the face of a woman.

In a writer of less genius than Emily Brontë Heathcliff would never have found his match; would never have found his mate, his equal, his twin-soul.

It needed the imagination of one who had both Heathcliff and Cathy in her to dig them both out of the same granite rock, covered with yellow gorse and purple ling, and to hurl them into one another's arms.

From the moment when they inscribed their initials upon the walls of that melancholy room, to the moment when, with a howl like a madman, Heathcliff drags her from her grave, their affiliation is desperate and absolute.

This is a love which passes far beyond all sensuality, far beyond all voluptuous pleasure. They get little good of their love, these two—little solace and small comfort.

But one cannot conceive their wishing to change their lot with any happier lovers. They are what they are, and they are prepared to endure what fate shall send them.

When Cathy admits to the old servant that she intends to marry Linton because Heathcliff was unworthy of her and would drag her down, "I love Linton," she says—"but *I am* Heathcliff!" And this *"I am* Heathcliff" rings in our ears as the final challenge to a chaotic pluralistic world full of cynical disillusionment, of the desperate spirit of which Emily Brontë was made.

The wild madness of such love—passing the love of men and women—may seem to many readers the mere folly of an insane dream.

Emily Brontë—as she was bound to do—tosses them forth, that inhuman pair, upon the voyaging homeless wind; tosses them forth, free of their desperation, to wander at large, ghosts of their own undying passions, over the face of the rainswept moors. But to most quiet and sceptical souls such an issue of the drama contradicts the laws of nature. To most patient slaves of destiny the end of the ashes of these fierce flames is to mingle placidly with the dark earth of those misty hills and find their release in nothing more tragic than the giving to the roots of the heather and the bracken a richer soil wherein to grow.

None of us know! None of us can ever know! It is enough that in this extraordinary story the wild strange link which once and again in the history of a generation binds so strangely two persons together, almost as though their association were the result of some aeon-old everlasting Recurrence, is once more thrown into tragic relief and given the tender beauty of an austere imagination.

Not every one can feel the spell of Emily Brontë or care for her work. To some she must always remain too ungracious, too savage, too uncompromising. But for those who have come to care for her, she is a wonderful and a lovely figure; a figure whose full significance has not even yet been sounded, a figure with whom we must come more and more to associate that liberation of what we call love from the mere animalism of sexual passion, which we feel sometimes, and in our rarer moments, to be one of the richest triumphs of the spirit over the flesh.

It may be that Emily Brontë is right. It may be that a point can be reached—perhaps is already being reached in the lives of certain individuals—where sexual passion is thus surpassed and transcended by the burning of a flame more intense than any which lust can produce.

It may be that the human race, as time goes on, will follow closer and closer this ferocious and spiritual girl in tearing aside the compromises of our hesitating timidity and plunging into the ice-cold waters of passions so keen and translunar as to have become chaste. It may be so—and, on the other hand, it may be that the old sly earth-gods will hold their indelible sway over us until the "baseless fabric" of this vision leaves "not a rack behind"! In any case, for our present purpose, the reading of Emily Brontë strengthens us in our recognition that the only wisdom of life consists in leaving all the doors of the universe open.

Cursed be they who close any doors! Let that be our literary as it is our philosophical motto.

Little have we gained from books, little from our passionate following in the steps of the great masters, if, after all, we only return once more to the narrow prejudices of our obstinate personal convictions.

From ourselves we cannot escape; but we can, unfortunately, hide ourselves from ourselves. We can hide ourselves "full-fathom-five" under our convictions and our principles. We can hide ourselves under our theories and our philosophies. It is only now and again, when, by some sudden devastating flash, some terrific burst of the thunder of the great gods, the real lineaments of what we are show up clearly for a moment in the dark mirror of our shaken consciousness.

It is well not to let the memory of those moments pass altogether away.

The reading of the great authors will have been a mere epicurean pastime if it has not made us recognise that what is important in our life is something that belongs more closely to us than any opinion we have inherited or any theory we have gained or any principle we have struggled for.

It will have been wasted if it has not made us recognise that in the moments when these outward things fall away, and the true self, beyond the power of these outward things, looks forth defiantly, tenderly, pitifully upon this huge strange world, there are intimations and whispers of something beyond all that the philosophers have ever dreamed, hidden in the reservoirs of being and ready to touch us with their breath.

Our reading of these noble writings will have been no more than a gracious entertainment if we have not come to see that the enormous differences of their verdicts prove conclusively that no one theory, no one principle, can cover the tremendous field. But such reading will have had but a poor effect if because of this radical opposition in the voices reaching us we give up our interest in the great quest.

For it is upon our retaining our interest that the birthright of our humanity depends.

We shall never find what we seek; that is certain enough. We should be gods, not men, if we found it. But we should be less than men, and beasts—if we gave up the interest of the search, the tremulous vibrating interest, which, like little waves of ether, hovers over the cross-roads where all the great ways part.

Something outside ourselves drives us on to seek it—this evasive solution of a riddle that seems eternal—and when, weary with the effort of refusing this or the other premature solution, weary with the effort of suspending our judgment and standing erect at that parting of the ways, we long in our hearts to drift at leisure down one of the many soothing streams, it is only the knowledge that it is not our intrinsic inmost self that so collapses and yields up the high prerogative of doubt, but some lesser self in us, some tired superficial self, which keeps us back from that betrayal. The courage with which Emily Brontë faced life, the equanimity with which she faced death, were in her case closely associated with the quiet desolate landscape which surrounded her. As my American poet says, it is only in the country that we can look upon these fatal necessities and see them as they are. To be born and to die fall into their place when we are living where the smell of the earth can reach us.

There will always be a difference between those who come from the country and those who come from the town; and if a time ever arrives when the cities of men so cover the earth that there will be room no longer for any country-bred persons in our midst, something will in that hour pass away forever from art and literature, and, I suspect, from philosophy too.

For you cannot acquire this quality by any pleasant trips through picturesque scenery. It is either in you or it is not in you. You either have the slow, tenacious, humorous, patient, imaginative instincts of the country-born; or you have the smart, quick, clever, witty, fanciful, lively, receptive, caustic turn of mind of those bred in the great cities.

We all come to the town, "some in rags and some in jags and some in velvet gowns"; but the country-born always recognises the country-born, and there is a natural affinity between them.

I suspect that those who have behind them no local, provincial traditions will find it difficult to understand Emily Brontë.

She did not deal in elaborate description; but the earth-mould smells sweet, and the roots of the reeds of the pond-rushes show wavering and dim in the dark water, and "through the hawthorn blows the cold wind," and the white moon drifts over the sombre furze-covered hills; and all these things have passed into her style and have formed her style, and all these things are behind the tenacity with which she endures life, and behind the immense mysterious hope with which, while regarding all human creeds as "unutterably vain," she falls back so fiercely upon that "amor intellectualis Dei" which is the burning fire in her own soul.

> —"Thou, thou art being and breath;
> And what thou art can never be destroyed!"

An Excerpt From
Suspended Judgments
- Essays on Books and Sensations, 1916

"JANE EYRE" AND "WUTHERING HEIGHTS"

BY VIRGINIA WOOLF

Of the hundred years that have passed since Charlotte Brontë was born, she, the centre now of so much legend, devotion, and literature, lived but thirty-nine. It is strange to reflect how different those legends might have been had her life reached the ordinary human span. She might have become, like some of her famous contemporaries, a figure familiarly met with in London and elsewhere, the subject of pictures and anecdotes innumerable, the writer of many novels, of memoirs possibly, removed from us well within the memory of the middle-aged in all the splendour of established fame. She might have been wealthy, she might have been prosperous. But it is not so. When we think of her we have to imagine some one who had no lot in our modern world; we have to cast our minds back to the 'fifties of the last century, to a remote parsonage upon the wild Yorkshire moors. In that parsonage, and on those moors, unhappy and lonely, in her poverty and her exaltation, she remains for ever.

These circumstances, as they affected her character, may have left their traces on her work. A novelist, we reflect, is bound to build up his structure with much very perishable material which begins by lending it reality and ends by cumbering it with rubbish. As we open Jane Eyre once more we cannot stifle the suspicion that we shall find her world of imagination as antiquated, mid-Victorian, and out of date as the parsonage on the moor, a place only to be visited by the curious, only preserved by the pious. So we open Jane Eyre; and in two pages every doubt is swept clean from our minds.

Folds of scarlet drapery shut in my view to the right hand; to the left were the clear panes of glass, protecting, but not separating me from the drear November day. At intervals, while turning over the leaves of my book, I studied the aspect of that winter afternoon. Afar, it offered a pale blank of mist and cloud; near, a scene of wet lawn and storm-beat shrub, with ceaseless rain sweeping away wildly before a long and lamentable blast.

There is nothing there more perishable than the moor itself, or more subject to the sway of fashion than the "long and lamentable blast". Nor is this exhilaration short-lived. It rushes us through the entire volume, without giving us time to think, without letting us lift our eyes from the page. So intense is our absorption that if some one moves in the room the movement seems to take place not there but up in Yorkshire. The writer has us by the hand, forces us along her road, makes us see what she sees, never leaves us for a moment or allows us to forget her. At the end we are steeped through and through with the genius, the vehemence, the indignation of Charlotte Brontë. Remarkable faces, figures of strong outline and gnarled feature have flashed upon us in passing; but it is through her eyes that we have seen them. Once she is gone, we seek for them in vain. Think of Rochester and we have to think of Jane Eyre. Think of the moor, and again there is Jane Eyre. Think of the drawing-room,11even, those "white carpets on which seemed laid brilliant garlands of flowers", that "pale Parian mantelpiece" with its Bohemia glass of "ruby red" and the "general blending of snow and fire"— what is all that except Jane Eyre?

11 Charlotte and Emily Brontë had much the same sense of colour. " . . . we saw — ah! it was beautiful — a splendid place carpeted with crimson, and crimson-covered chairs and tables, and a pure white ceiling bordered by gold, a shower of glass drops hanging in silver chains from the centre, and shimmering with little soft tapers" (Wuthering Heights). "Yet it was merely a

very pretty drawing-room, and within it a boudoir, both spread with white carpets, on which seemed laid brilliant garlands of flowers; both ceiled with snowy mouldings of white grapes and vine leaves, beneath which glowed in rich contrast crimson couches and ottomans; while the ornaments on the pale Parian mantelpiece were of sparkling Bohemia glass, ruby red; and between the windows large mirrors repeated the general blending of snow and fire" (Jane Eyre).

The drawbacks of being Jane Eyre are not far to seek. Always to be a governess and always to be in love is a serious limitation in a world which is full, after all, of people who are neither one nor the other. The characters of a Jane Austen or of a Tolstoi have a million facets compared with these. They live and are complex by means of their effect upon many different people who serve to mirror them in the round. They move hither and thither whether their creators watch them or not, and the world in which they live seems to us an independent world which we can visit, now that they have created it, by ourselves. Thomas Hardy is more akin to Charlotte Brontë in the power of his personality and the narrowness of his vision. But the differences are vast. As we read Jude the Obscure we are not rushed to a finish; we brood and ponder and drift away from the text in plethoric trains of thought which build up round the characters an atmosphere of question and suggestion of which they are themselves, as often as not, unconscious. Simple peasants as they are, we are forced to confront them with destinies and questionings of the hugest import, so that often it seems as if the most important characters in a Hardy novel are those which have no names. Of this power, of this speculative curiosity, Charlotte Brontë has no trace. She does not attempt to solve the problems of human life; she is even unaware that such problems exist; all her force, and it is the more tremendous for being constricted, goes into the assertion, "I love", "I hate", "I suffer".

For the self-centred and self-limited writers have a power denied the more catholic and broad-minded. Their impressions are close packed and strongly stamped between their narrow walls. Nothing issues from their minds which has not been marked with their own impress. They learn little from other writers, and what they adopt they cannot assimilate. Both Hardy and Charlotte Brontë appear to have founded their styles upon a stiff and decorous journalism. The staple of their prose is awkward and unyielding. But both with labour and the most obstinate integrity, by thinking every thought until it has subdued words to itself, have forged for themselves a prose which takes the mould of their minds entire; which has, into the bargain, a beauty, a power, a swiftness of its own. Charlotte Brontë, at least, owed nothing to the reading of many books. She never learnt the smoothness of the professional writer, or acquired his ability to stuff and sway his language as he chooses. "I could never rest in communication with strong, discreet, and refined minds, whether male or female", she writes, as any leader-writer in a provincial journal might have written; but gathering fire and speed goes on in her own authentic voice "till I had passed the outworks of conventional reserve and crossed the threshold of confidence, and won a place by their hearts' very hearthstone". It is there that she takes her seat; it is the red and fitful glow of the heart's fire which illumines her page. In other words, we read Charlotte Brontë not for exquisite observation of character — her characters are vigorous and elementary; not for comedy — hers is grim and crude; not for a philosophic view of life — hers is that of a country parson's daughter; but for her poetry. Probably that is so with all writers who have, as she has, an overpowering personality, so that, as we say in real life, they have only to open the door to make themselves felt. There is in them some untamed ferocity perpetually at war with the accepted order of things which makes them desire to create instantly rather than to observe patiently. This very ardour, rejecting half shades and other minor impediments, wings its way past the daily conduct of ordinary people and allies itself with their more inarticulate passions. It makes them poets, or, if they choose to write in prose, intolerant of its restrictions. Hence it is that both Emily and Charlotte are always invoking the help of nature. They both feel the need of some more powerful symbol of the vast and slumbering passions in human nature than words or actions can convey. It is with a description of a storm that Charlotte ends her finest novel Villette. "The skies hang full and dark — a wrack sails from the west; the clouds cast themselves into strange forms." So she calls in nature to describe a state of mind which could not otherwise be expressed. But neither of the sisters observed nature accurately as Dorothy Wordsworth observed it, or painted it minutely as Tennyson painted it. They seized those aspects of the earth which were most akin to what they themselves felt or imputed to their characters, and so their storms, their moors, their lovely spaces of summer weather are not ornaments applied to decorate a dull page or display the writer's powers of observation — they carry on the emotion and light up the meaning of the book.

The meaning of a book, which lies so often apart from what happens and what is said and consists rather in some connection which things in themselves different have had for the writer, is necessarily hard to grasp. Especially this is so when, like the Brontës, the writer is poetic, and his meaning inseparable from his language, and itself rather a mood than a particular observation. Wuthering Heights is a more difficult book to understand than Jane Eyre, because Emily was a greater poet than Charlotte. When Charlotte wrote she said with eloquence and splendour and passion "I love", "I hate", "I suffer". Her experience, though more intense, is on a level with our own. But there is no "I" in Wuthering Heights. There are no governesses. There are no employers. There is love, but it is not the love of men and women. Emily was inspired by some more general conception. The impulse which urged her to create was not her own suffering or her own injuries. She looked out upon a world cleft into gigantic disorder and felt within her the power to unite it in a book. That gigantic ambition is to be felt throughout the novel — a struggle, half thwarted but of superb conviction, to say something through the mouths of her characters which is not merely "I love" or "I hate", but "we, the whole human race" and "you, the eternal powers . . . " the sentence remains unfinished. It is not strange that it should be so; rather it is astonishing that she can make us feel what she had it in her to say at all. It surges up in the half-articulate words of Catherine Earnshaw, "If all else perished and HE remained, I should still continue to be; and if all else remained and he were annihilated, the universe would turn to a mighty stranger; I should not seem part of it". It breaks out again in the presence of the dead. "I see a repose that neither earth nor hell can break, and I feel an assurance of the endless and shadowless hereafter — the eternity they have entered — where life is boundless in its duration, and love in its sympathy and joy in its fulness." It is this suggestion of power underlying the apparitions of human nature and lifting them up into the presence of greatness that gives the book its huge stature among other novels. But it was not enough for Emily Brontë to write a few lyrics, to utter a cry, to express a creed. In her poems she did this once and for all, and her poems will perhaps outlast her novel. But she was novelist as well as poet. She must take upon herself a more laborious and a more ungrateful task. She must face the fact of other existences, grapple with the mechanism of external things, build up, in recognisable shape, farms and houses and report the speeches of men and women who existed independently of herself. And so we reach these summits of emotion not by rant or rhapsody but by hearing a girl sing old songs to herself as she rocks in the branches of a tree; by watching the moor sheep crop the turf; by listening to the soft wind breathing through the grass. The life at the farm with all its absurdities and its improbability is laid open to us. We are given every opportunity of comparing Wuthering Heights with a real farm and Heathcliff with a real man. How, we are allowed to ask, can there be truth or insight or the finer shades of emotion in men and women who so little resemble what we have seen ourselves? But even as we ask it we see in Heathcliff the brother that a sister of genius might have seen; he is impossible we say, but nevertheless no boy in literature has a more vivid existence than his. So it is with the two Catherines; never could women feel as they do or act in their manner, we say. All the same, they are the most lovable women in English fiction. It is as if she could tear up all that we know human beings by, and fill these unrecognisable transparences with such a gust of life that they transcend reality. Hers, then, is the rarest of all powers. She could free life from its dependence on facts; with a few touches indicate the spirit of a face so that it needs no body; by speaking of the moor make the wind blow and the thunder roar.

AN EXCERPT FROM
The Common Reader, 1916

CHARLOTTE AND EMILY BRONTË

BY ALICE MEYNELL

The controversy here is with those who admire Charlotte Brontë throughout her career. She altered greatly. She did, in fact, inherit a manner of English that had been strained beyond restoration, fatigued beyond recovery, by the "corrupt following" of Gibbon; and there was within her a sense of propriety that caused her to conform. Straitened and serious elder daughter of her time, she kept the house of literature. She practised those verbs, to evince, to reside, to intimate, to peruse. She wrote "communicating instruction" for teaching; "an extensive and eligible connexion"; "a small competency"; "an establishment on the Continent"; "It operated as a barrier to further intercourse"; and of a child (with a singular unfitness with childhood) "For the toys he possesses he seems to have contracted a partiality amounting to affection." I have been already reproached for a word on Gibbon written by way of parenthesis in the course of an appreciation of some other author. Let me, therefore, repeat that I am writing of the corrupt following of that apostle and not of his own style. Gibbon's grammar is frequently weak, but the corrupt followers have something worse than poor grammar. Gibbon set the fashion of "the latter" and "the former." Our literature was for at least half a century strewn with the wreckage of Gibbon. "After suppressing a competitor who had assumed the purple at Mentz, he refused to gratify his troops with the plunder of the rebellious city," writes the great historian. When Mr. Micawber confesses "gratifying emotions of no common description" he conforms to a lofty and a distant Gibbon. So does Mr. Pecksniff when he says of the copper-founder's daughter that she "has shed a vision on my path refulgent in its nature." And when an author, in a work on "The Divine Comedy," recently told us that Paolo and Francesca were to receive from Dante "such alleviation as circumstances would allow," that also is a shattered, a waste Gibbon, a waif of Gibbon. For Johnson less than Gibbon inflated the English our fathers inherited; because Johnson did not habitually or often use imagery, whereas Gibbon did use habitual imagery, and such use is what deprives a language of elasticity, and leaves it either rigid or languid, oftener languid. Encumbered by this drift and refuse of English, Charlotte Brontë yet achieved the miracle of her vocabulary. It is less wonderful that she should have appeared out of such a parsonage than that she should have arisen out of such a language.

A re-reading of her works is always a new amazing of her reader who turns back to review the harvest of her English. It must have been with rapture that she claimed her own simplicity. And with what a moderation, how temperately, and how seldom she used her mastery! To the last she has an occasional attachment to her bonds; for she was not only fire and air. In one passage of her life she may remind us of the little colourless and thrifty hen-bird that Lowell watched nest-building with her mate, and cutting short the flutterings and billings wherewith he would joyously interrupt the business; Charlotte's nesting bird was a clergyman. He came, lately affianced, for a week's visit to her parsonage, and she wrote to her friend before his arrival: "My little plans have been disarranged by an intimation that Mr.—is coming on Monday"; and afterwards, in reference to her sewing, "he hindered me for a full week."

In alternate pages *Villette* is a book of spirit and fire, and a novel of illiberal rancour, of ungenerous, uneducated anger, ungentle, ignoble. In order to forgive its offences, we have to remember in its author's favour not her pure style set free, not her splendour in literature, but rather the immeasurable sorrow of her life. To read of that sorrow again is to open once more a wound which most men perhaps, certainly most women, received into their hearts in childhood. For the Life of Charlotte Brontë is one of the first books of biography put into the hands of a child, to whom *Jane Eyre* is allowed only in passages. We are young when we first hear in what narrow beds "the three are laid"—the two sisters and the brother—and in what a bed of living insufferable memories the one left lay alone, reviewing the hours of their death—alone in the sealed house that was only less narrow than their graves. The rich may set apart and dedicate a room, the poor change their street, but Charlotte Brontë, in the close captivity of the fortunes of mediocrity, rested in the chair that had been her dying sister's, and held her melancholy bridals in the dining room that had been the scene of terrible and reluctant death.

But closer than the conscious house was the conscious mind. Locked with intricate wards within the unrelaxing and unlapsing thoughts of this lonely sister, dwelt a sorrow inconsolable. It is well for the perpetual fellowship of mankind that no child should read this life and not take therefrom a perdurable scar, albeit her heart was somewhat frigid towards childhood, and she died before her motherhood could be born.

Mistress of some of the best prose of her century, Charlotte Brontë was subject to a Lewes, a Chorley, a Miss Martineau: that is, she suffered what in Italian is called *soggezione* in their presence. When she had met six minor contemporary writers—by-products of literature—at dinner, she had a headache and a sleepless night. She writes to her friend that these contributors to the quarterly press are greatly feared in literary London, and there is in her letter a sense of tremor and exhaustion. And what nights did the heads of the critics undergo after the meeting? Lewes, whose own romances are all condoned, all forgiven by time and oblivion, who gave her lessons, who told her to study Jane Austen? The others, whose reviews doubtless did their proportionate part in still further hunting and harrying the tired English of their day? And before Harriet Martineau she bore herself reverently. Harriet Martineau, albeit a woman of masculine understanding (we may imagine we hear her contemporaries give her the title), could not thread her way safely in and out of two or three negatives, but wrote—about this very Charlotte Brontë: "I did not consider the book a coarse one, though I could not answer for it that there were no traits which, on a second leisurely reading, I might not dislike." Mrs. Gaskell quotes the passage with no consciousness of anything amiss.

As for Lewes's vanished lesson upon the methods of Jane Austen, it served one only sufficient purpose. Itself is not quoted by anyone alive, but Charlotte Brontë's rejoinder adds one to our little treasury of her incomparable pages. If they were twenty, they are twenty-one by the addition of this, written in a long-neglected letter and saved for us by Mr. Shorter's research, for I believe his is the only record: "What sees keenly, speaks aptly, moves flexibly, it suits her to study; but what throbs fast and full, though hidden, what blood rushes through, what is the unseen seat of life and the sentient target of death—that Miss Austen ignores."

When the author of *Jane Eyre* faltered before six authors, more or less, at dinner in London, was it the writer of her second-class English who was shy? or was it the author of the passages here to follow?—and therefore one for whom the national tongue was much the better? There can be little doubt. The Charlotte Brontë who used the English of a world long corrupted by "one good custom"—the good custom of Gibbon's Latinity grown fatally popular—could at any time hold up her head amongst her reviewers; for her there was no sensitive interior solitude in that society. She who cowered was the Charlotte who made Rochester recall "the simple yet sagacious grace" of Jane's first smile; she who wrote: "I looked at my love; it shivered in my heart like a suffering child in a cold cradle"; who wrote: "To see what a heavy lid day slowly lifted, what a wan glance she flung upon the hills, you would have thought the sun's fire quenched in last night's floods." This new genius was solitary and afraid, and touched to the quick by the eyes and voice of judges. In her worse style there was no "quick." Latin-English, whether scholarly or unscholarly, is the mediate tongue. An unscholarly Latin-English is proof against the world. The scholarly Latin-English wherefrom it is disastrously derived is, in its own nobler measure, a defence against more august assaults than those of criticism. In the strength of it did Johnson hold parley with his profounder sorrows—hold parley (by his phrase), make terms (by his definition), give them at last lodging and entertainment after sentence and treaty.

And the meaner office of protection against reviewers and the world was doubtless done by the meaner Latinity. The author of the phrase "The child contracted a partiality for his toys" had no need to fear any authors she might meet at dinner. Against Charlotte Brontë's sorrows her worse manner of English never stands for a moment. Those vain phrases fall from before her face and her bared heart. To the heart, to the heart she took the shafts of her griefs. She tells them therefore as she suffered them, vitally and mortally. "A great change approached. Affliction came in that shape which to anticipate is dread; to look back on, grief. My sister Emily first declined. Never in all her life had she lingered over any task that lay before her, and she did not linger now. She made haste to leave us." "I remembered where the three were laid—in what narrow, dark dwellings." "Do you know this place? No, you never saw it; but you recognize the nature of these trees, this foliage—the cypress, the willow, the yew. Stone crosses like these are not unfamiliar to you, nor are these dim garlands of everlasting flowers. Here is the place." "Then the watcher approaches the patient's pillow, and sees a new and strange moulding of the familiar features, feels at once that the insufferable moment draws nigh." In the same passage comes another single word of genius, "the sound that so wastes our strength." And, fine as "wastes," is the "wronged" of another sentence—"some wronged and fettered wild beast or bird."

It is easy to gather such words, more difficult to separate the best from such a mingled page as that on "Imagination": "A spirit, softer and better than human reason, had descended with quiet flight to the waste"; and "My hunger has this good angel appeased with food sweet and strange"; and "This daughter of Heaven remembered me to-night; she saw me weep, and she came with comfort; 'Sleep,' she said, 'sleep sweetly—I gild thy dreams.'" "Was this feeling dead? I do not know, but it was buried. Sometimes I thought the tomb unquiet."

Perhaps the most "eloquent" pages are unluckily those wherein we miss the friction—friction of water to the oar, friction of air to the pinion—friction that sensibly proves the use, the buoyancy, the act of language. Sometimes an easy eloquence resembles the easy labours of the daughters of Danaus. To draw water in a sieve is an easy art, rapid and relaxed.

But no laxity is ever, I think, to be found in her brief passages of landscape. "The keen, still cold of the morning was succeeded, later in the day, by a sharp breathing from the Russian wastes; the cold zone sighed over the temperate zone and froze it fast." "Not till the destroying angel of tempest had achieved his perfect work would he fold the wings whose waft was thunder, the tremor of whose plumes was storm." "The night is not calm: the equinox still struggles in its storms. The wild rains of the day are abated: the great single cloud disappears and rolls away from Heaven, not passing and leaving a sea all sapphire, but tossed buoyant before a continued, long-sounding, high-rushing moonlight tempest. . . No Endymion will watch for his goddess to-night: there are no flocks on the mountains." See, too, this ocean: "The sway of the whole Great Deep above a herd of whales rushing through the livid and liquid thunder down from the frozen zone." And this promise of the visionary Shirley: "I am to be walking by myself on deck, rather late of an August evening, watching and being watched by a full harvest moon: something is to rise white on the surface of the sea, over which that moon mounts silent, and hangs glorious. . . I think I hear it cry with an articulate voice. .

. I show you an image fair as alabaster emerging from the dim wave."

Charlotte Brontë knew well the experience of dreams. She seems to have undergone the inevitable dream of mourners—the human dream of the Labyrinth, shall I call it? the uncertain spiritual journey in search of the waiting and sequestered dead, which is the obscure subject of the "Eurydice" of Coventry Patmore's Odes. There is the lately dead, in exile, remote, betrayed, foreign, indifferent, sad, forsaken by some vague malice or neglect, sought by troubled love astray.

In Charlotte Brontë's page there is an autumnal and tempestuous dream. "A nameless experience that had the hue, the mien, the terror, the very tone of a visitation from eternity. . . Suffering brewed in temporal or calculable measure tastes not as this suffering tasted." Finally, is there any need to cite the passage of *Jane Eyre* that contains the avowal, the vigil in the garden? Those are not words to be forgotten. Some tell you that a fine style will give you the memory of a scene and not of the recording words that are the author's means. And others again would have the phrase to be remembered foremost. Here, then, in *Jane Eyre*, are both memories equal. The night is perceived, the phrase is an experience; both have their place in the reader's irrevocable past. "Custom intervened between me and what I naturally and inevitably loved." "Jane, do you hear that nightingale singing in the wood?" "A waft of wind came sweeping down the laurel walk, and trembled through the boughs of the chestnut; it wandered away to an infinite distance. . . The nightingale's voice was then the only voice of the hour; in listening I again wept."

* * * * *

Whereas Charlotte Brontë walked, with exultation and enterprise, upon the road of symbols, under the guidance of her own visiting genius, Emily seldom went out upon those far avenues. She was one who practised imagery sparingly. Her style had the key of an inner prose which seems to leave imagery behind in the way of approaches—the apparelled and arrayed approaches and ritual of literature—and so to go further and to be admitted among simple realities and antitypes.

Charlotte Brontë also knew that simple goal, but she loved her imagery. In the passage of *Jane Eyre* that tells of the return to Thornfield Hall, in ruins by fire, she bespeaks her reader's romantic attention to an image which in truth is not all golden. She has moments, on the other hand, of pure narrative, whereof each word is such a key as I spoke of but now, and unlocks an inner and an inner plain door of spiritual realities. There is, perhaps, no author who, simply telling what happened, tells it with so great a significance: "Jane, did you hear that nightingale singing in the wood?" and "She made haste to leave us." But her characteristic calling is to images, those avenues and temples oracular, and to the vision of symbols.

You may hear the poet of great imagery praised as a great mystic. Nevertheless, although a great mystical poet makes images, he does not do so in his greatest moments. He is a great mystic, because he has a full vision of the mystery of realities, not because he has a clear invention of similitudes.

> Of many thousand kisses the poor last,

and

> Now with his love, now in the colde grave

are lines on the yonder side of imagery. So is this line also:

> Sad with the promise of a different sun,

and

> Piteous passion keen at having found,
> After exceeding ill, a little good.

Shakespeare, Chaucer and Patmore yield us these great examples. Imagery is for the time when, as in these lines, the shock of feeling (which must needs pass, as the heart beats and pauses) is gone by:

> Thy heart with dead winged innocence filled,
> Even as a nest with birds,
> After the old ones by the hawk are killed.

I cite these lines of Patmore's because of their imagery in a poem that without them would be insupportably close to spiritual facts; and because it seems to prove with what a yielding hand at play the poet of realities holds his symbols for a while. A great writer is both a major and a minor mystic, in the self-same poem; now suddenly close to his mystery (which is his greater moment) and anon making it mysterious with imagery (which is the moment of his most beautiful lines).

The student passes delighted through the several courts of poetry, from the outer to the inner, from riches to more imaginative riches, and from decoration to more complex decoration; and prepares himself for the greater opulence of the innermost chamber. But when he crosses the last threshold he finds this mid-most sanctuary to be a hypaethral temple, and in its custody and care a simple earth and a space of sky.

Emily Brontë seems to have a nearly unparalleled unconsciousness of the delays, the charms, the pauses and preparations of imagery. Her strength does not dally with the parenthesis, and her simplicity is ignorant of those rites. Her lesser work, therefore, is plain narrative, and her greater work is no more. On the hither side—the daily side—of imagery she is still a strong and solitary writer; on the yonder side she has written some of the most mysterious passages in all plain prose.

And with what direct and incommunicable art! "'Let me alone, let me alone,' said Catherine. 'If I've done wrong, I'm dying for it. You left me too . . . I forgive you. Forgive me!' 'It is hard to forgive, and to look at those eyes and feel those wasted hands,' he answered. 'Kiss me again, and don't let me see your eyes! I forgive what you have done to me. I love my murderer—but *yours*! How can I?' They were silent, their faces hid against each other, and washed by each other's tears." "So much the worse for me that I am strong," cries Heathcliff in the same scene. "Do I want to live? What kind of living will it be when you—Oh God, would you like to live with your soul in the grave?"

Charlotte Brontë's noblest passages are her own speech or the speech of one like herself acting the central part in the dreams and dramas of emotion that she had kept from her girlhood— the unavowed custom of the ordinary girl by her so splendidly avowed in a confidence that comprised the world. Emily had no such confessions to publish. She contrived—but the word does not befit her singular spirit of liberty, that knew nothing of stealth—to remove herself from the world; as her person left no pen-portrait, so her "I" is not heard here. She lends her voice in disguise to her men and women; the first narrator of her great romance is a young man, the second a servant woman; this one or that among the actors takes up the story, and her great words sound at times in paltry mouths. It is then that for a moment her reader seems about to come into her immediate presence, but by a fiction she denies herself to him. To a somewhat trivial girl (or a girl who would be trivial in any other book, but Emily Brontë seems unable to create anything consistently meagre)— to Isabella Linton she commits one of her most memorable passages, and one which has the rare image, one of a terrifying little company of visions amid terrifying facts: "His attention was roused, I saw, for his eyes rained down tears among the ashes. . . The clouded windows of hell flashed for a moment towards me; the fiend which usually looked out was so dimmed and drowned." But in Heathcliff's own speech there is no veil or circumstance. "I'm too happy; and yet I'm not happy enough. My soul's bliss kills my body, but does not satisfy itself." "I have to remind myself to breathe, and almost to remind my heart to beat." "Being alone, and conscious two yards of loose earth was the sole barrier between us, I said to myself: 'I'll have her in my arms again.' If she be cold, I'll think it is this north wind that chills me; and if she be motionless, it is sleep." What art, moreover, what knowledge, what a fresh ear for the clash of repetition; what a chime in that phrase: "I dreamt I was sleeping the last sleep by that sleeper, with my heart stopped, and my cheek frozen against hers."

Emily Brontë was no student of books. It was not from among the fruits of any other author's labour that she gathered these eminent words. But I think I have found the suggestion of this action of Heathcliff's—the disinterment. Not in any inspiring ancient Irish legend, as has been suggested, did Emily Brontë find her incident; she found it (but she made, and did not find, its beauty) in a mere costume romance of Bulwer Lytton, whom Charlotte Brontë, as we know, did not admire. And Emily showed no sign at all of admiration when she did him so much honour as to borrow the action of his studio-bravo.

Heathcliff's love for Catherine's past childhood is one of the profound surprises of this unparalleled book; it is to call her childish ghost—the ghost of the little girl—when she has been a dead adult woman twenty years that the inhuman lover opens the window of the house on the Heights. Something is this that the reader knew not how to look for. Another thing known to genius and beyond a reader's hope is the tempestuous purity of those passions. This wild quality of purity has a counterpart in the brief passages of nature that make the summers, the waters, the woods, and the windy heights of that murderous story seem so sweet. The "beck" that was audible beyond the hills after rain, the "heath on the top of Wuthering Heights" whereon, in her dream of Heaven, Catherine, flung out by angry angels, awoke sobbing for joy; the bird whose feathers she—delirious creature—plucks from the pillow of her deathbed ("This—I should know it among a thousand—it's a lapwing's. Bonny bird; wheeling over our heads in the middle of the moor. It wanted to get to its nest, for the clouds had touched the swells and it felt rain coming"); the only two white spots of snow left on all the moors, and the brooks brim-full; the old apple-trees, the smell of stocks and wallflowers in the brief summer, the few fir-trees by Catherine's window-bars, the early moon—I know not where are landscapes more exquisite and natural. And among the signs of death where is any fresher than the window seen from the garden to be swinging open in the morning, when Heathcliff lay within, dead and drenched with rain?

None of these things are presented by images. Nor is that signal passage wherewith the book comes to a close. Be it permitted to cite it here again. It has taken its place, it is among the paragons of our literature. Our language will not lapse or derogate while this prose stands for appeal: "I lingered . . . under that benign sky; watched the moths fluttering among the heath and harebells, listened to the soft wind breathing through the grass, and wondered how anyone could ever imagine unquiet slumbers for the sleepers in that quiet earth."

Finally, of Emily Brontë's face the world holds only an obviously unskilled reflection, and of her aspect no record worth having. Wild fugitive, she vanished, she escaped, she broke away, exiled by the neglect of her contemporaries, banished by their disrespect outlawed by their contempt, dismissed by their indifference. And such an one was she as might rather have pronounced upon these the sentence passed by Coriolanus under sentence of expulsion; she might have driven the world from before her face and cast it out from her presence as he condemned his Romans: "*I* banish you."

AN EXCERPT FROM
Hearts of Controversy, 1918

THE CHALLENGE OF THE BRONTËS

BY EDMUND WILLIAM GOSSE

Although I possess in no degree the advantage which so many of the members of your society enjoy in being personally connected with the scenes and even, perhaps, with the characters associated with the Brontë family, I cannot begin my little address to you to-day without some invocation of the genius of the place. We meet at Dewsbury because the immortal sisters were identified with Dewsbury. Is it then not imperative that for whatever picture of them I may endeavour to present before you this afternoon, Dewsbury should form the background? Unfortunately, however, although in the hands of a skilful painter the figures of the ladies may glow forth, I fear that in the matter of taking Dewsbury as the background some vagueness and some darkness are inevitable. In the biographies of Mrs. Gaskell and of Mr. Clement Shorter, as well as in the proceedings of your society, I have searched for evidences of the place Dewsbury took in the lives of the Brontës. What I find—I expect you to tell me that it is not exhaustive—is this. Their father, the Rev. Patrick Brontë, was curate here from 1809 to 1811. In 1836, when Charlotte was twenty, Miss Wooler transferred her school from Roe Head to Heald's House at the top of Dewsbury Moor. In this school, where Charlotte had been a pupil since 1831, she was now a governess, and a governess she remained until early in 1838. In April of that year Miss Wooler was taken ill and Charlotte was for a little while in charge. Then there was an explosion of temper, of some kind, and Charlotte went back to Haworth.

That, then, in the main, is the limit of what the scrupulous Muse of history vouchsafes to tell us about Charlotte Brontë's relation to Dewsbury. But it also supplies us with one or two phrases which I cannot bring myself to spare you. In January 1838, Charlotte reviews her experience at Dewsbury Moor; "I feel," she says, "in nothing better, nothing humbler nor purer." Again, in 1841, after there had passed time enough to mellow her exacerbations, she continues to express herself with vigour. Miss Wooler is making overtures to Charlotte and Emily to take over the school at Heald's House; perhaps a place might be found for Anne as well. Miss Wooler, one of the kindest of women, is most thoughtful, most conciliatory. Charlotte will have none of the idea; she puts it roughly from her. Of Dewsbury she has nothing to say but that "it is a poisoned place for me." This is all we know of Charlotte's relation to Dewsbury, yet nothing, you will tell me, in Froude's phrase, to what the angels know. Well, I must be frank with you and say that I am afraid the angels have been inclined to record exceedingly little of Charlotte Brontë's residence in your inoffensive neighbourhood. I have to paint a background to my picture, and I find none but the gloomiest colours. They have to be what the art-critics of the eighteenth century called "sub-fusc." But it is not the fault of Dewsbury, it is the fault, or the misfortune, of our remarkable little genius. She was here, in this wholesome and hospitable vicinity, for several months, during which time "she felt in nothing better, neither humbler nor purer," and looking back upon it, she had to admit that it was "a poisoned place" to her.

I cannot help fancying that you will agree with me, that on such an occasion as the present, and especially when dealing with a group of writers about whom so much as has been said as about the Brontës, it is wise not to cover too wide a ground, but to take, and keep to, one aspect of the subject. Our little excursion into the history seems to have given us, under the heading "Dewsbury," a rather grim text, from which, nevertheless, we may perhaps extract some final consolation. Let me say at the outset that for the grimness, for the harshness, Dewsbury is not at all to blame. I fancy that if, in the years from 1836 to 1838, the Brontë girls had been visitors to Kubla Khan, and had been fed on honey by his myrmidons at Xanadu, that pleasure-dome would yet have been "poisoned" to them. It was not poverty, and cold, and the disagreeable position of a governess, it was not the rough landscape of your moors, nor its lack of southern amenity which made Charlotte wretched here. It was not in good Miss Wooler, nor in the pupils, nor in the visitors at Heald's House that the mischief lay, it was in the closed and patient crater of Charlotte's own bosom. And I am almost persuaded that, if you had lived in Dewsbury sixty-five years ago, you would have heard on very quiet days a faint subterranean sound which you would never have been able to guess was really the passion, furiously panting, shut up in the heart of a small, pale governess in Heald's House schoolroom.

If you accuse me of fatalism, I am helpless in your hands, for I confess I do not see how it could be otherwise, and do scarcely wish that it could have been. Let us not be too sentimental in this matter. Figures in literature are notable and valuable to us for what they give us. The more personal and intense and definite that is, the greater the gift, the more strenuous the toil and the more severe the initiation which lead to its expression. The Brontës had a certain thing to learn to give; what that was we shall presently try to note. But whatever we find it to be, we start with allowing that it was extremely and boldly original. It was not to be mastered by lying upon padded sofas and toying with a little Berlin wool-work. It involved pain, resistance, a stern revision of things hitherto taken for granted. The secrets which they designed to wring from nature and from life were not likely to be revealed to the self-indulgent and the dilettante. The sisters had a message from the sphere of indignation and revolt. In order that they should learn it as well as teach it, it was necessary that they should arrive on the scene at an evil hour for their own happiness. *Jane Eyre* and *Shirley* and *Villette* could not have been written unless, for long years, the world had been "a poisoned place" for Charlotte Brontë.

It has been excellently said by Mrs. Humphry Ward that in many respects, and to the very last, the Brontës challenge no less than they attract us. This is an aspect which, in the midst of rapturous modern heroine-worship, we are apt to forget. Thackeray, who respected the genius of the family, and was immensely kind to the author of *Jane Eyre*, never really felt comfortable in her company. We know how he stole out of his own front-door, and slipped away into the night to escape her. "A very austere little person," he called her, and we may put what emphasis on the austerity we will. I feel sure that any maladroit "white-washing of Charlotte" will tend, sooner or later, good-natured though it may be, in a failure to comprehend what she really was, in what her merit consisted, what the element in her was that, for instance, calls us here together nearly half a century after she completed her work and passed away. Young persons of genius very commonly write depressing books; since, the more vivid an unripe creature's impression of life is, the more acute is its distress. It is only extremely stupid Sunday-school children who shout in chorus, "We are so happy, happy, happy!" Genius thrown naked, with exposed nerves, on a hard indifferent world, is never "happy" at first. Earth is a "poisoned place" to it, until it has won its way and woven its garments and discovered its food.

But in the case of Charlotte Brontë, unhappiness was more than juvenile fretfulness. All her career was a revolt against conventionality, against isolation, against irresistible natural forces, such as climate and ill-health and physical insignificance. Would this insubmissive spirit have passed out of her writings, as it passed, for instance, out of those of George Sand? I am not sure, for we see it as strongly, though more gracefully and skilfully expressed, in *Villette* as in the early letters which her biographers have printed. Her hatred of what was commonplace and narrow and obvious flung her against a wall of prejudice, which she could not break down. She could only point to it by her exhausting efforts; she could only invite the generation which succeeded her to bring their pickaxes to bear upon it. Hence, to the very last, she seems, more than any other figure in our literature, to be forever ruffled in temper, for ever angry and wounded and indignant, rejecting consolation, crouched like a sick animal in the cavern of her own quenchless pride. This is not an amiable attitude, nor is it historically true that this was Charlotte Brontë's constant aspect. But I will venture to say that her amiabilities, her yielding moods, are really the unessential parts of her disposition, and that a certain admirable ferocity is the notable feature of her intellectual character.

Her great heart was always bleeding. Here at Dewsbury, in the years we are contemplating, the hemorrhage was of the most doleful kind, for it was concealed, suppressed, it was an inward flow. When once she became an author the pain of her soul was relieved. She said, in 1850, looking back on the publication of the hapless first volume of poems, "The mere effort to succeed gave a wonderful zest to existence." Then, a little later, when no one had paid the slightest attention to the slender trio of maiden voices, "Something like the chill of despair began to invade their hearts." With a less powerful inspiration, they must have ceased to make the effort; they must have succumbed in a melancholy oblivion. But they were saved by the instinct of a mission. It was not their private grief which primarily stirred them. What urged them on was the dim consciousness that they gave voice to a dumb sense of the suffering of all the world. They had to go on working; they had to pursue their course, though it might seem sinister or fatal; their business was to move mankind, not to indulge or please it. They "must be honest; they must not varnish, soften, or conceal."

What Charlotte Brontë was learning to do in her grim and, let us admit it, her unlovely probation on Dewsbury Moor, was to introduce a fresh aspect of the relations of literature to life. Every great writer has a new note; hers was—defiance. All the aspects in which life presented itself to her were distressing, not so much in themselves as in herself. She rebelled against the outrages of poverty, and she drank to its dregs the cup of straitened circumstances. She was proud, as proud as Lucifer, and she was forced into positions which suppleness and cheerfulness might have made tolerable, if not agreeable. She wrung from these positions their last drop of bitterness. A very remarkable instance of this may be found in her relation to the Sidgwick family, who, by universal report, were generous, genial, and unassuming. To Charlotte Brontë these kindly, if somewhat commonplace folk, grew to seem what a Turkish pasha seems to the inhabitants of a Macedonian village. It was not merely the surroundings of her life—it was life itself, in its general mundane arrangements, which was intolerable to her. She fretted in it, she beat her wings against its bars, and she would have done the same if those bars had been of gold, and if the fruits of paradise had been pushed to her between them. This, I think, is why the expression of her anger seems too often disproportionate, and why her irony is so apt to be preposterous. She was born to resist being caged in any form. Her defiance was universal, and often it was almost indiscriminate.

Do not let us presume to blame this insubmission. Still less let us commit the folly of minimising it. A good cheerful little Charlotte Brontë, who thought the best of everybody, who gaily took her place without a grudging sigh, whose first aim was to make those about her happy and to minister to their illusions, would have been a much more welcome inmate of Miss Wooler's household than the cantankerous governess whom nobody could please, whose susceptibilities were always on edge, whose lonely arrogance made her feared by all but one or two who timidly persisted in loving her. But such a paragon of the obvious virtues would have passed as the birds pass and as the flowers. She would have left no mark behind. She would never have enriched the literature of England by one of its master-evidences of the force of human will. She would never have stirred hundreds of thousands of consciences to a wholesome questioning of fate and their own souls.

Let us endeavour to pursue the inquiry a few steps further. It is impossible to separate the ethical conditions of an author's mind from the work that he produces. The flower requires the soil; it betrays in its colour and its perfume the environment of its root. The moral constitution of the writer is reflected in the influence of the written page. This is the incessant contention; on one hand the independence of art asserts itself; on the other, it is impossible to escape from the implicit influence of conduct upon art. There have been few writers of any age in whom this battle raged more fiercely than it did in Charlotte Brontë. Her books, and those of her sisters, seem anodyne enough to-day; to readers of a sensitive species they seemed, when they were published, as dangerous as *Werther* had been, as seductive as the *Nouvelle Heloïse*. The reason of this was, in the main, the spirit of revolt which inspired them. There was something harsh and glaring in their landscape; there was that touch of Salvator Rosa which one of their earliest critics observed in them. But more essential was the stubbornness, the unflinching determination to revise all accepted formulas of conduct, to do this or that, not because it was usual to do it, but because it was rational, and in harmony with human nature.

Into an age which had become almost exclusively utilitarian, and in which the exercise of the imagination, in its real forms, was sedulously discountenanced, Charlotte Brontë introduced passion in the sphere of prose fiction, as Byron had introduced it in the sphere of verse thirty years earlier. It was an inestimable gift; it had to come to us, from Charlotte Brontë or another, to save our literature from a decline into triviality and pretension. But she suffered, as Byron had suffered, in the direct ratio of her originality. If a writer employs passion in an age which has ceased to recognise it as one of the necessities of literary vitality he is safe to be accused of perverting his readers. Balzac says, "When nothing else can be charged against an author, the reproach of immorality is thrown at his head." When we study the record of the grim life of the sisters at Haworth, like that of three young soldiers round a camp-fire with the unseen enemy prowling in the darkness just out of their sight—when we think of the strenuous vigil, the intractable and indomitable persistence, the splendour of the artistic result—we may console ourselves in our anger at the insults they endured, by reflecting how little they cared. And their noble indifference to opinion further endears them to us. We may repeat of them all what Charlotte in a letter once said of Emily, "A certain harshness in her powerful and peculiar character only makes me cling to her more."

This insubmissiveness, which was the unconscious armour given to protect her against the inevitable attacks of fortune, while, on the other hand, it was the very sign-manual of Charlotte's genius, was, on the other, a drawback from which she did not live long enough to emancipate her nature. It is responsible for her lack of interest in what is delicate and complex; it excused to herself a narrowness of vision which we are sometimes tempted to find quite distressing. It is probably the cause of a fault that never quits her for long, a tendency to make her characters express themselves with a lyrical extravagance which sometimes comes close to the confines of rodomontade. Charlotte Brontë never arrives at that mastery of her material which permits the writer to stand apart from his work, and sway the reader with successive tides of emotion while remaining perfectly calm himself. Nor is she one of those whose visible emotion is nevertheless fugitive, like an odour, and evaporates, leaving behind it works of art which betray no personal agitation. On the contrary, her revolt, her passion, all the violence of her sensibility, are present on her written page, and we cannot read it with serenity or with a merely captious curiosity, because her own eager spirit, immortal in its active force, seems to throb beside it.

The aspect of Charlotte Brontë which I have tried to indicate to you to-day, and which I have sketched thus hastily and slightly against the background of her almost voiceless residence in Dewsbury, is far from being a complete or unique one. I offer it to you only as a single facet of her wonderful temperament, of the rich spectacle of her talent. I have ventured to propose it, because, in the multiplication of honours and attentions, the tendency to deify the human, to remove those phenomena of irregularity which are the evidence of mortal strength, grows irresistible, and we find ourselves, unconsciously, substituting a waxen bust, with azure eyes and golden hair, for the homely features which (if we could but admit it) so infinitely better match the honest stories. Let us not busy ourselves to make excuse for our austere little genius of the moors. Let us be content to take her exactly as she was, with her rebellion and her narrowness, her angers and her urgencies, perceiving that she had to be this sorrowful offspring of a poisoned world in order to clear the wells of feeling for others, and to win from emancipated generations of free souls the gratitude which is due to a precursor.

AN EXCERPT FROM
Some Diversions of a Man of Letters, 1919

www.ingramcontent.com/pod-product-compliance
Lightning Source LLC
Chambersburg PA
CBHW022116090426
42743CB00008B/869